an earth and space science unit for high-ability learners in grade 3

Dig It!

Dig It!

Project Clarion Primary Science Units
Funded by the Jacob K. Javits Program, United States Department of Education

The College of William and Mary
School of Education
Center for Gifted Education
P.O. Box 8795
Williamsburg, VA 23187-8795

Co-Principal Investigators: Bruce A. Bracken & Joyce VanTassel-Baska
Project Directors: Lori C. Bland, Tamra Stambaugh, & Valerie Gregory
Unit Developers: Elizabeth Crawford, Heather M. French, & Bronwyn MacFarlane
Unit Revision: Lori C. Bland

Edited by Lacy Compton
Production Design by Marjorie Parker

ISBN-13: 978-1-59363-395-0
ISBN-10: 1-59363-395-5

Prufrock Press Inc.
P.O. Box 8813
Waco, TX 76714-8813
Phone: (800) 998-2208
Fax: (800) 240-0333
http://www.prufrock.com

Contents

Part I: Unit Overview

Introduction to the Clarion Units

The Project Clarion Science Units for Primary Grades introduce young students to science concepts, science reasoning, and scientific investigation processes. Macroconcepts, such as systems or change, help students connect understanding of science content and processes. The units use a hands-on, constructivist approach that allows children to build their knowledge base and their skills as they explore science topics through play and planned investigations. Students are engaged in creative and critical thinking, problem finding and solving, process skill development, and communication opportunities. Conceptual understanding is reinforced as units strengthen basic language and mathematical concepts, including quantity, direction, position, comparison, colors, letter identification, numbers, counting, size, social awareness, texture, material, shape, time, and sequence.

Introduction to the *Dig It!* Unit

Dig It!, a third-grade Earth and space science unit, engages students in a scenario-based approach to investigating the effects of humans on the environment, the importance of Earth's natural resources, and sound conservation practices. The unit focuses on the macroconcept of change to help students understand how natural resources change over time, how the environment changes, and how humans change the environment and impact natural resources. The *Dig It!* unit builds upon students' prior knowledge by providing opportunities to relate local examples of environmental pollution and conservation with hands-on scientific experiments and demonstrations. The first lesson in the unit introduces students to the role of a scientist. Students assume the role of environmental scientists working on a team to conduct investigations about natural resources, pollution, and conservation. While working to understand the role of natural resources and the impact humans have on the environment and natural resources, the team members seek to answer questions such as "How can we plan a prevention garden?"

Curriculum Framework

The curriculum framework (see Table 1) developed for the Project Clarion science units is based on the Integrated Curriculum Model (ICM), which posits the relatively equal importance of teaching to high-level content, higher order processes and resultant products, and important concepts and issues. The model represents a research-based set of differentiated curricular and instructional approaches found appropriate for high-ability learners (VanTassel-Baska, 1986; VanTassel-Baska & Little, 2003). The framework serves several important functions:

1. The curriculum framework provides scaffolding for the central concept of change, the scientific research process, and the content of the units.
2. The curriculum framework also provides representative statements of advanced, complex, and sophisticated learner outcomes. It demonstrates how a single set of outcomes for all can be translated appropriately for high-ability learners yet can remain accessible to other learners.
3. The curriculum framework provides a way for readers to get a snapshot view of the key emphases of the curriculum in direct relation to each other. The

Table 1
Project Clarion Curriculum
Framework for Science Units

Goal	Student Outcomes The student will be able to:
1. Develop concepts related to understanding the world of science.	• Provide examples, illustrations, and salient features of important science and math concepts. • Categorize and/or classify various concepts. • Identify counterexamples of specific concepts. • Create definitions and generalizations about various concepts.
2. Develop an understanding of the macroconcept of change as it relates to science content goals.	• Understand that change is everywhere. • Demonstrate the impact of time on change. • Articulate the nature of natural versus manmade change. • Evaluate the nature of change (predictable or random) in selected phenomena.
3. Develop knowledge of selected content topics in Earth science.	• Identify sources of energy on Earth, including sunlight, water, and wind. • Distinguish between renewable and nonrenewable natural energy sources. • Describe how human activity affects the quality of air, water, and habitats. • Describe how conservation and resource renewal protect the quality and quantity of natural resources. • Provide examples of human dependency on several major sources of energy found on Earth. • Articulate that fossil fuels are formed from decayed plants and animals. • Articulate how soil provides support and nutrients for plants. • Identify components of soil, including rock, clay, silt, and sand. • Identify topsoil as the upper soil surface and a natural product of the subsoil bedrock. • Distinguish between subsoil and bedrock as layers of soil under topsoil and understand that topsoil is formed over a long period of time by the action of water. • Analyze how soil is created over time as weather, water, and living things break down rocks.
4. Develop interrelated science process skills.	• Make observations. • Ask questions. • Learn more. • Design and conduct an experiment. • Create meaning. • Tell others what was found.
5. Develop critical thinking skills.	• Describe problematic situations or issues. • Define relevant concepts. • Identify different points of view in situations or issues. • Describe evidence or data supporting a scientific question. • Draw conclusions based on data (making inferences). • Predict consequences.
6. Develop creative thinking skills.	• Develop fluency when naming objects and ideas. • Develop flexible thinking. • Elaborate on ideas presented in oral or written form. • Create products that replicate and extend conceptual understanding.
7. Develop curiosity and interest in the world of science.	• Express reactions about discrepant events. • Ask meaningful questions about science topics. • Articulate ideas of interest about science. • Demonstrate persistence in completing science tasks.

model also provides a way to traverse the elements individually through the continuum of grade levels.

Moreover, the framework may be used to implement the William and Mary units and to aid in new curriculum development based on science reform recommendations.

Standards Alignment

Each lesson was aligned to the appropriate National Science Education Standards (NSES), Content Standards: K–4 (Center for Science, Mathematics, and Engineering Education, CSMEE, 1996). Table 2 presents detailed information on the alignment between the NSES Content Standards and fundamental concepts within the unit lessons.

Macroconcept

The macroconcept for this unit is *change*. A concept paper on change is included in Appendix A. The second lesson in this unit introduces the concept of change. Students are asked to brainstorm examples of change, categorize their examples, identify "nonexamples" of the concept, and make generalizations about the concept (Taba, 1962). The generalizations about change incorporated into this unit of study include:
- Change is everywhere.
- Change relates to time.
- Change can be natural or manmade.
- Change may be random or predictable.

The concept of change is integrated throughout the unit lessons and deepens students' understanding of natural resources and how resources may change. Students examine the relationship of important ideas and issues about natural resources through application of the concept generalizations. This higher level thinking enhances the students' ability to "think like a scientist." More information about concept development is provided in Appendix B: Teaching Models.

Key Science Concepts

By the end of this unit, students will understand that:
1. Sources of energy on Earth include sunlight, water, and wind.
2. Some natural energy resources are renewable and some are not.
3. Human activity affects the quality of air, water, and habitat.
4. Conservation and resource renewal protect the quality and quantity of natural resources.
5. Humans depend on several major sources of energy found on Earth.
6. Fossil fuels are formed from decayed plants and animals.
7. Soil provides support and nutrients for plants.
8. Rock, clay, silt, sand, and humus are components of soil.
9. Topsoil is the upper soil surface and a natural product of the subsoil and bedrock.
10. Subsoil and bedrock are layers of soil under the topsoil from which topsoil is formed over a long period of time by the action of water.
11. Over time, weather, water, and living things help break down rocks and create soil.

Practice in using concept maps supports students' learning as they begin to build upon known concepts (Novak & Gowin, 1984). Students begin to add new concepts to their initial understandings of a topic and to make new connections between concepts. The use of concept maps within the lessons also helps teachers to recognize

Table 2
Dig It! Alignment to National Science Education Standards

Standard	Fundamental Concepts	Unit Lesson
Content Standard A: Abilities necessary to do scientific inquiry	• Ask a question about objects, organisms, and events in the environment. • Plan and conduct a simple investigation. • Employ simple equipment and tools to gather data and extend the senses. • Use data to construct a reasonable explanation. • Communicate investigations and explanations.	1, 2, 3, 4, 5, 6, 7, 8, 9, 10, 11, 12, 13, 14
Content Standard A: Understanding about scientific inquiry	• Scientific investigations involve asking and answering a question and comparing the answer with what scientists already know about the world. • Scientists use different kinds of investigations depending on the questions they are trying to answer. Types of investigations include: describing objects, events, and organisms; classifying them; and doing a fair test (experimenting). • Simple instruments, such as magnifiers, thermometers, and rulers, provide more information than scientists obtain using only their senses. • Scientists develop explanations using observations (evidence) and what they already know about the world (scientific knowledge). Good explanations are based on evidence from investigations. • Scientists make the results of their investigations public; they describe the investigation in ways that enable others to repeat the investigation. • Scientists review and ask questions about the results of other scientists' work.	1, 2, 3, 4, 5, 6, 7, 8, 9, 10, 11, 12, 13, 14
Content Standard B: Position and motion of objects	• An object's motion can be described by tracing and measuring its position over time.	3, 13, 14
Content Standard B: Light, heat, electricity, and magnetism	• Light travels in a straight line until it strikes an object. Light can be reflected by a mirror, refracted by a lens, or absorbed by an object.	7, 13, 14
Content Standard C: The characteristics of organisms	• Organisms have basic needs. For example, animals need air, water, and food; plants require air, water, nutrients, and light. Organisms can survive only in environments in which their needs can be met. The world has many different environments, and distinct environments support the life of different types of organisms.	9, 13, 14
Content Standard C: Organisms and environments	• An organism's pattern of behavior is related to the nature of that organism's environment, including the kinds and numbers of other organisms present, the availability of food and resources, and the physical characteristics of the environment. When the environment changes, some plants and animals survive and reproduce and others die or move to a new location. • All organisms cause changes in the environment where they live. Some of these changes are detrimental to the organism or other organisms, whereas others are beneficial. • Humans depend on their natural and constructed environments. Humans change environments in ways that can be either beneficial or detrimental for themselves and other organisms.	4, 5, 6, 10, 11, 12, 13, 14

Standard	Fundamental Concepts	Unit Lesson
Content Standard D: Properties of Earth materials	• Earth materials are solid rocks and soils, water, and the gases of the atmosphere. The varied materials have different physical and chemical properties that make them useful in different ways (e.g., as building materials, as sources of fuel, or for growing the plants we use as food). Earth materials provide many of the resources that humans use. • Soils have properties of color and texture, capacity to retain water, and ability to support the growth of many kinds of plants, including those in our food supply.	8, 9, 13, 14
Content Standard D: Changes in Earth and sky	• The surface of the Earth changes. Some changes are due to slow processes, such as erosion and weathering, and some changes are due to rapid processes, such as landslides, volcanic eruptions, and earthquakes.	10, 13, 14
Content Standard E: Abilities of technological design	• Identify a simple problem. • Propose a solution. • Implement the proposed solution. • Evaluate a product or design. • Communicate a problem, design, and solution.	13, 14
Content Standard E: Understanding about science and technology	• People have always had questions about their world. Science is one way of answering questions and explaining the natural world. • Scientists and engineers often work in teams with different individuals doing different things that contribute to the results. This understanding focuses primarily on teams working together and secondarily on the combination of scientist and engineer teams. • Women and men of all ages, backgrounds, and groups engage in a variety of scientific and technological work. • Tools help scientists make better observations, measurements, and equipment for investigation. They help scientists see, measure, and do things that they could not otherwise see, measure, and do.	1
Content Standard F: Personal health	• Safety and security are basic needs of humans. Safety involves freedom from danger, risk, or injury. Security involves feelings of confidence, and lack of anxiety and fear. Student understandings include following safety rules for home and school, preventing abuse and neglect, avoiding injury, knowing whom to ask for help, and when and how to say no.	Science Safety Lesson
Content Standard F: Types of resources	• Resources are things that we get from the living and nonliving environment to meet the needs and wants of a population. • Some resources are basic materials, such as air, water, and soil; some are produced from basic resources, such as food, fuel, and building materials; and some resources are nonmaterial, such as quiet places, beauty, security, and safety. • The supply of many resources is limited. If used, resources can be extended through recycling and decreased use.	4, 5, 6, 7, 11, 13, 14
Content Standard F: Changes in environments	• Changes in environments can be natural or influenced by humans. Some changes are good, some are bad, and some are neither good nor bad. Pollution is a change in the environment that can influence the health, survival, or activities of organisms, including humans. • Some environmental changes occur slowly, and others occur rapidly. Students should understand the different consequences of changing environments in small increments over long periods as compared with changing environments in large increments over short periods.	10, 11, 12, 13, 14
Content Standard G: Science as a human endeavor	• Men and women have made a variety of contributions throughout the history of science and technology. • Although men and women using scientific inquiry have learned much about the objects, events, and phenomena in nature, much more remains to be understood. Science will never be finished. • Many people choose science as a career and devote their entire lives to studying it. Many people derive great pleasure from doing science.	1

students' conceptual frameworks so that instruction can be adapted as necessary. More information on strategies for using concept mapping, as well as a list of concept mapping practice activities, is provided in Appendix B.

Each Project Clarion unit contains a science concept map (see Figure 1) that displays the essential understandings and the connections students should be able to make as a result of their experiences within the unit. This overview may be useful as a classroom poster that teachers and students can refer to throughout the unit.

In addition to the concept map, teachers also will notice references to a "word wall" in the unit. The word wall is suggested for use in the classroom while teaching the unit. On this wall, teachers will post or write words (and their definitions) that go along with the lessons. Use the definitions listed in the Unit Glossary for the word wall; you also can use additional vocabulary from the lessons that may be unfamiliar to the students on the word wall. At the end of the unit, teachers are instructed to assign words from the word wall to student groups for an activity that involves students creating word demonstrations. Teachers can assess students' understanding of each word or concept by the quality of understanding demonstrated in students' presentations. A list of materials needed for the unit is provided in Appendix C.

Scientific Investigation and Reasoning

The Wheel of Scientific Investigation and Reasoning contains the specific processes involved in scientific inquiry that guide students' thinking and actions. To read more about these processes and suggestions for implementing the wheel into this unit's lessons, see Appendix B.

The following lessons utilize the Wheel of Scientific Investigation and Reasoning:
- Lessons 3 and 7, which help students explore the six components of scientific investigation including: Make Observations, Ask Questions, Learn More, Design and Conduct Experiments, Create Meaning, and Share Results.
- Lessons 4–14, which provide opportunities for students to apply one or more components of scientific investigation and culminate with an in-depth scientific investigation.

Students use the wheel to analyze aspects of an investigation or to plan an investigation. Scientific investigation concepts within the lessons include:
- *Make Observations*: Scientists use their senses as well as instruments to note details, identify similarities and differences, and record changes in phenomena.
- *Ask Questions*: Scientists use information from their observations about familiar objects or events to develop important questions that spark further investigation.
- *Learn More*: Scientists carefully review what is known about a topic and determine what additional information must be sought.
- *Design and Conduct Experiments*: Scientists design an experiment, which is a fair test of a hypothesis or prediction and is intended to answer a question for a scientific investigation.
- *Create Meaning*: Scientists carefully gather and record data from an experiment, then analyze the data.
- *Share Results*: Scientists communicate findings from an experiment, including a clear description of the question, the hypothesis or prediction, the experiment that was conducted, the data that were collected and how they were analyzed, and the conclusions and inferences that were made from the experiment.

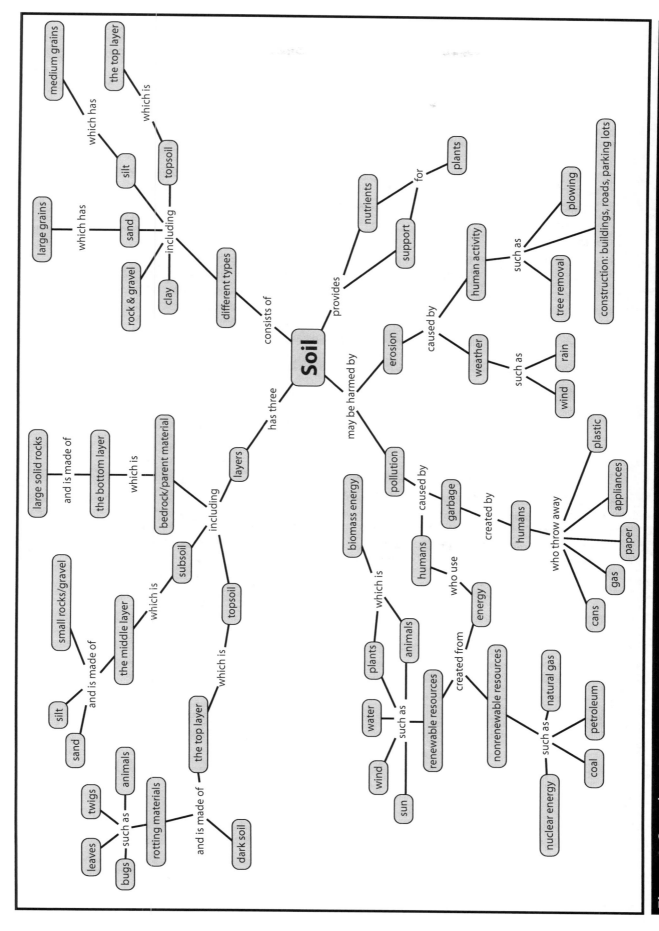

Figure 1. Sample unit concept map.

9

Assessment

The unit includes performance-based assessments for students to complete at the beginning (preassessment) and end (postassessment) of the unit. There are three pre- and postassessments, which assess conceptual understanding, science content knowledge, and application of the scientific investigation process. The preassessment provides baseline data that teachers can use to adjust instructional plans for individual students or groups of students. Preteaching activities accompany selected preassessments.

The postassessment is administered at the completion of the unit and provides valuable information about students' mastery of the targeted objectives and the National Science Education Standards. A rubric is used to score each pre- and postassessment. The pre- and postassessments and dimensions of learning scored for each task include:

- *A macroconcept template, which requires students to draw or write about the macroconcept.* Conceptual understanding is scored on the pre- and postassessments based on the number of appropriate examples of the macroconcept, the elements of the macroconcept, types of the macroconcept listed, and generalizations about the macroconcept.
- *Concept maps, which assess students' content knowledge.* Students are given a prompt for creating a concept map about the unit topic. Understanding of key science concepts is scored on the pre- and postassessments based on the number of appropriate hierarchical levels, propositions, and examples listed.
- *An experimental design template, which requires students to plan an experiment with a given scientific research question.* Students are asked to design an experiment to investigate a question. Students are scored on the pre- and postassessments on their ability to write a prediction or hypothesis, list materials needed for the experiment, list the steps of the experiment in order, and develop a plan to organize data for collection and interpretation.

Teachers also should note that assessment "Look Fors" are designated in the first section of each lesson plan. The "Look Fors" provide a means for teachers to assess student learning in each lesson. The "Look Fors" are linked to the macroconcept generalizations, key science concepts, and scientific processes identified in each lesson. Teachers can develop checklists for the "Look Fors" or may make informal observations, for example.

Teacher's Guide to Content

The definitions of key science concepts taught in the unit are described below. A unit glossary and list of content resources also are included.

Conservation

Conservation is the attempt to manage natural resources by reducing their use, eliminating waste, or using resources more efficiently.

Types and Uses of Natural Resources

Like all life on Earth, human beings are dependent on the natural environment for survival. Obviously, we rely on natural resources such as air, soil, water, plants, and animals to provide our most basic needs. We also rely on less apparent natural resources to maintain our standard of living. For instance, the Mineral Information Institute estimated that the average American baby born in 2007 will require the mining of more than 3.7 million pounds of metals and minerals over the course of its life. These materials will be used to provide products such as building materials, fuel, and road surfaces. Fossil fuels are particularly important natural resources. Most of the fossil fuels currently being taken from the Earth are used primarily as fuel, but the byproducts are used in the manufacture of almost every product on the market today, including shampoo, plastic, and food additives.

Renewable and Nonrenewable Resources

Supplies of many other resources can be replenished. These renewable resources fall into two categories: conditionally renewable and perpetually renewable. Conditionally renewable resources might be depleted in the short run but can renew themselves over time if used carefully. Examples of conditionally renewable resources include forests and stocks of fish and game. On the other hand, some resources, such as light and wind, exist in constant supply no matter how they are used by humans. These resources are perpetually renewable. However, many of the resources we use are nonrenewable; current supplies cannot be replaced. Nonrenewable resources include natural gas and metals.

Renewable and Nonrenewable Energy Sources

One special category of natural resources is the group used for the production of energy. Like other natural resources, energy sources can be nonrenewable or renewable.

Nonrenewable energy sources include coal, petroleum, natural gas, liquefied petroleum gas (LPG), and nuclear energy. Nuclear energy is energy released by the fusing or breaking up of atoms. Nuclear power plants require uranium, a metal, to create the nuclear reaction. Like all metals, uranium is a nonrenewable resource.

A large percentage of our need for power is met through the use of nonrenewable energy sources, even though renewable sources of power are available. Power can be generated using solar energy, wind, water, geothermal energy, or biomass energy. Geothermal power is generated using heat energy from below the Earth's surface. Biomass is plant or animal material that can be burned for fuel, such as wood from trees, rice husks, or manure. Although these energy sources can be replenished, they have other drawbacks that keep them from being ideal solutions to our energy problems. For instance, burning biomass causes air pollution, making solar cells generates toxic byproducts, and the dams required for hydroelectric power can have a negative effect on the surrounding environment.

Pollution

There are four major types of pollution: chemical, thermal, organic, and ecological. Pollution can be caused by humans, but it also can occur naturally.

Chemical pollution, the introduction of toxins into an ecosystem, is caused by humans. Examples of chemical pollution include factories draining waste into a river or cars releasing exhaust fumes into the air. One well-known type of chemical pollution is an oil spill. Oil spills can require massive cleanup efforts. The spill must first be contained within barriers. The reprocessed oil may then be burned so that only the residue remains, or it can be skimmed off of the water's surface. Even after the oil has been removed from land or water, plants and animals may still be affected. Volunteers at oil spill sites often spend much of their time trying to save the lives of animals unable to fly or breathe because they are coated with oil. Oil spills often kill or injure plants and animals that live in water.

Thermal pollution is pollution that causes temperatures in an area to stray from normal. This type of pollution is caused by humans. Power plants releasing steam into the atmosphere, thereby raising the surrounding air temperature, would be an example of thermal pollution. Scientists are concerned about another type of thermal pollution: global warming. This is caused by the "greenhouse effect." The greenhouse effect describes a rise in temperature caused by the release of gases such as carbon dioxide and methane into the atmosphere. These gases keep solar energy from escaping into space, resulting in warmer temperatures.

Organic pollution happens when too many nutrients enter an ecosystem. In aquatic systems, this can lead to excessive growth of algae and other organisms and a reduction in the amount of oxygen in the water, which causes fish to die. This type of pollution can occur naturally or be caused by humans. Runoff of agricultural fertilizers is a significant source of manmade organic pollution.

The most common form of natural pollution is ecological pollution. Natural examples of this type of pollution include droppings from birds, introducing new plants to an area, or high tides moving salt water to habitats normally protected from tides by storm or drought. Human activity can cause ecological pollution as well. Damming rivers and streams can dramatically alter an ecosystem; deforestation increases soil erosion.

Sources of pollution can be divided into two categories: point and nonpoint sources. Point sources enter the environment from a single area, such as a factory pipe that releases toxins directly into a river or lake. Nonpoint sources are spread over a large area and might include the waste generated by a city or fertilizer runoff from a large agricultural area.

Environmental Protection

As we have learned more about the effect humans have on our planet, people have begun to take action in order to protect the environment. Governments have enacted laws to protect wilderness areas and restrict the amount of pollutants released in the environment. Some United States laws intended to protect the environment are the Clean Air Act (1970), the Endangered Species Act (1973), and the Clean Water Act (1977). Governments also are working to solve local problems such as waste disposal. Much of the waste produced by humans is buried in landfills, which are large tracts of land blocked off from the surrounding environment to prevent contamination. Although the design of landfills protects the surrounding environment from contamination by the trash, it also keeps the trash from biodegrading, or being broken down and returning to the soil. Because the waste in a landfill cannot biodegrade, landfills are simply filled up with more and more trash. Local governments deal with this problem in many ways, including encouraging citizens to recycle and approving projects that reclaim the landfill land for another purpose.

Individual citizens also can take steps to improve the health of the environment. Some people choose to join environmental groups such as Greenpeace, while others take steps such as recycling, walking or bicycling to work, and using renewable energy sources to heat their homes and businesses.

Unit Glossary

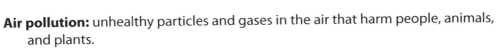

Air pollution: unhealthy particles and gases in the air that harm people, animals, and plants.

Bedrock: native consolidated rock underlying the Earth's surface.

Classify: to put things into groups according to their characteristics.

Clay: a type of sediment soil that has microscopic grains; feels slippery or sticky; when wet, holds together and can be rolled into a long, snake-shaped strand.

Conservation: the protection of valuable things, especially forests, wildlife, and natural resources.

Erosion: the gradual wearing away of a substance by water or wind.

Experiment: a scientific test to try out a theory or to see the effect of something.

Fossil fuel: coal, oil, or natural gas formed from the remains of prehistoric plants.

Habitat: the place and conditions in which plants or animals live.

Humus: rotting material—plants and animals—in topsoil.

Hydroelectric: electrical energy produced by running water.

Hypothesis: a temporary prediction that can be tested about how a scientific investigation or experiment will turn out.

Natural environment: the natural world of the land, sea, and air.

Natural resources: naturally occurring materials that can be used by living organisms to meet specific needs.

Nonrenewable energy: a resource available in limited amounts.

Observation: the careful watching of someone or something.

Pollution: harmful materials that damage or contaminate the air, water, and soil, such as toxic chemicals, engine exhaust, and industrial waste.

Renewable energy: power from sources that can never be used up, such as wind, waves, and the sun.

Sand: largest grains of soil; feels gritty; when wet, holds together but crumbles easily.

Sea level: the average level of the surface of the ocean, used as a starting point from which to measure the height (measured above sea level) or depth of any place.

Silt: medium-sized grains of sediment; feels smooth and silky between fingers but gritty between teeth; when wet, holds together and does not crumble easily, but cannot be rolled into a long, snake-shaped strand.

Solar energy: energy from the sun that can be used for heating and generating electricity.

Subsoil: lower middle layer of soil; contains larger pieces of rock and less decaying material than topsoil.

Teaching Resources

Required Resources (Used in Relevant Lessons)

Bang, M. (1997). *Common ground: The water, earth, and air we share*. New York: Blue Sky Press.

Berger, M. (2006). *Oil spill!* Boston: Houghton Mifflin.

Bunting, E. (1993). *Someday a tree*. New York: Clarion Books.

Deedy, C. A. (1994). *Agatha's feather bed: Not just another wild goose story*. Atlanta, GA: Peachtree.

Jeffers, S. (2002). *Brother eagle, sister sky*. New York: Puffin.

Lehn, B. (1999). *What is a scientist?* Minneapolis, MN: Millbrook Press.

McKinney, B. (1998). *A drop around the world*. Nevada City, CA: Dawn Publications.

Showers, P. (1994). *Where does the garbage go?* New York: HarperCollins.

Silverstein, S. (1974). Sarah Cynthia Sylvia Stout would not take the garbage out. In *Where the sidewalk ends: The poems and drawings of Shel Silverstein* (pp. 70–71). New York: HarperCollins.

Additional Resources

Amos, J. (1994). *Waste and recycling*. Austin, TX: Steck-Vaughn.

Baer-Brown, L., & Rhein, B. (1995). *Earth keepers: A sourcebook for environmental issues and action*. San Francisco: Mercury House.

Ballard, C. (2005). *The search for better conservation*. Milwaukee, WI: Gareth Stevens.

Bang, M. (2004). *My light*. New York: Blue Sky Press.

Calhoun, Y. (2005). *Conservation*. Philadelphia: Chelsea House.

Cothram, H. (2002). *Energy alternatives: Opposing viewpoints*. San Diego, CA: Greenhaven Press.

DuTemple, L. A. (1999). *Oil spills*. San Diego, CA: Lucent Books.

Galko, F. (2004). *Earth friends at play: Reduce, reuse, recycle*. Chicago: Heinemann.

Galko, F. (2004). *Earth friends at school: Reduce, reuse, recycle*. Chicago: Heinemann.

Gallant, R. A. (2003). *Resources: Nature's riches*. New York: Benchmark Books.

Hanrahan, C. (2007). *Global resources: Opposing viewpoints*. San Diego, CA: Greenhaven Press.

Klare, M. T. (2001). *Resource wars: The new landscape of global conflict*. New York: Holt.

Kramer, S. P. (1987). *How to think like a scientist: Answering questions by the scientific method*. New York: HarperCollins.

Russell, W. (1994). *Oil, coal, and gas: From this Earth*. Vero Beach, FL: Rourke.

Saunders, N., & Chapman, S. (2004). *Fossil fuel*. Chicago: Heinemann.

Schaefer, C. L. (2005). *Cool time song*. New York: Viking.

Stewart, M. (2002). *Soil*. Chicago: Heinemann.

Van Allsburg, C. (1990). *Just a dream*. Boston: Houghton Mifflin.

Useful Web Sites

California Energy Commission. (2002). *Energy story*. Retrieved from http://www.energyquest.ca.gov/story

Chesapeake Bay Program Office. (n.d.). *Chesapeake Bay Program: A watershed partnership.* Retrieved from http://www.chesapeakebay.net

Energy Information Administration. (n.d.). *Official energy statistics from the U.S. government.* Retrieved from http://eia.doe.gov

Freudenrich, C. (n.d.). *How landfills work.* Retrieved from http://howstuffworks.com/landfill.htm

Mineral Information Institute. (2005). *Everything we have and everything we use comes from our natural resources.* Retrieved from http://www.mii.org

National Renewable Energy Laboratory. (2008). *Learning about renewable energy.* Retrieved from http://www.nrel.gov/learning

United States Department of Energy. (2009). *Energy efficiency and renewable energy.* Retrieved from http://www.eere.energy.gov

United States Environmental Protection Agency. (2008). *Municipal solid waste.* Retrieved from http://www.epa.gov/osw/nonhaz/municipal

Part II: Lesson Plans

Lesson Plans

Overview of Lessons

Preteaching Lesson: Science Safety

Preassessment Directions for the Teacher

Lesson 1: What Is a Scientist?

Lesson 2: What Is Change?

Lesson 3: What Scientists Do

Lesson 4: Preservation Park

Lesson 5: Natural Resources, Part I

Lesson 6: Natural Resources, Part II

Lesson 7: Renewable Energy Resources

Lesson 8: What Is Soil, Anyway?

Lesson 9: Soil, Water, and Plants

Lesson 10: Soil Erosion

Lesson 11: Land Pollution: Garbage!

Lesson 12: Oil Spill!

Lesson 13: Planning Preservation Park

Lesson 14: Preservation Park Planning Committee

Lesson 15: Wrap It Up!

Postassessment Directions for the Teacher

Overview of Lessons

An overview of the lessons is provided in Table 3. The overview shows the primary emphasis of each lesson in the unit according to the macroconcept, key science concepts, or the scientific investigation process. Lessons also may have a secondary emphasis, which is listed in the planning section of each lesson.

Table 3
Overview of Lessons

Concept of Change	Scientific Process	Key Science Concepts
Preassessment		
	Lesson 1: What Is a Scientist?	
Lesson 2: What Is Change?		
	Lesson 3: What Scientists Do	
Lesson 4: Preservation Park		
		Lesson 5: Natural Resources, Part I
		Lesson 6: Natural Resources, Part II
	Lesson 7: Renewable Energy Resources	
		Lesson 8: What Is Soil, Anyway?
	Lesson 9: Soil, Water, and Plants	
Lesson 10: Soil Erosion		
	Lesson 11: Land Pollution: Garbage!	
	Lesson 12: Oil Spill!	
	Lesson 13: Planning Preservation Park	
Lesson 14: Preservation Park Planning Committee		
Lesson 15: Wrap It Up!		
Postassessment		

Lesson Plan Blueprint

The lesson plan blueprint is provided in Table 4. The blueprint shows for each lesson:
- the instructional purpose,
- generalizations about the macroconcept of change,
- key science concepts,
- scientific investigation skills and processes, and
- assessment "Look Fors."

Table 4
Lesson Plan Blueprint

Lesson Number	Title	Instructional Purposes	Change Generalizations	Key Science Concepts	Scientific Investigation Skills and Processes	Assessment "Look Fors" Students should be able to:
	Preassessment					
1	What Is a Scientist?	• To learn the characteristics of scientists and the investigation skills that scientists use.			• Make observations. • Ask questions. • Learn more. • Design and conduct experiments. • Create meaning. • Tell others what was found.	• Distinguish between scientists and nonscientists. • Identify scientific investigation processes used by scientists.
2	What Is Change?	• To develop an understanding of the concept of change. • To make generalizations about change.	• Change is everywhere. • Change is related to time. • Change can be natural or manmade. • Change may be random or predictable.		• Make observations.	• Identify change. • Use the five senses to determine change. • Apply change generalizations appropriately to determine changes.
3	What Scientists Do	• To introduce the Wheel of Scientific Investigation and Reasoning. • To apply the steps of the scientific investigation processes described in the wheel to initiate an investigation of the power of the wind.	• Change is everywhere. • Change is related to time. • Change can be natural or manmade. • Change may be random or predictable.	• Sources of energy on Earth include sunlight, water, and wind. • Some natural energy resources are renewable and some are not.	• Make observations. • Ask questions. • Learn more. • Design and conduct experiments. • Create meaning. • Tell others what was found.	• Apply the steps of scientific investigation. • Interpret data from a data table.
4	Preservation Park	• To introduce students to a scenario they will be using throughout the unit to explore change, the key science concepts, and the scientific investigation process.	• Change is everywhere. • Change is related to time. • Change can be natural or manmade. • Change may be random or predictable.	• Sources of energy on Earth include sunlight, water, and wind. • Some natural energy resources are renewable and some are not. • Human activity affects the quality of air, water, and habitat. • Conservation and resource renewal protect the quality and quantity of natural resources. • Humans depend on several major sources of energy found on Earth.	• Ask questions. • Learn more.	• Apply change generalizations to our environment. • Draw inferences about environmental devastation and pollution.

Table 4, continued

Lesson Number	Title	Instructional Purposes	Change Generalizations	Key Science Concepts	Scientific Investigation Skills and Processes	Assessment "Look Fors" Students should be able to:
5, 6	Natural Resources, Parts I and II	• To introduce students to the concept of natural resources. • To explore the interrelationship between living creatures and the environment.	• Change is everywhere. • Change is related to time. • Change can be natural or manmade. • Change may be random or predictable.	• Sources of energy on Earth include sunlight, water, and wind. • Some natural energy resources are renewable and some are not. • Conservation and resource renewal protect the quality and quantity of natural resources. • Humans depend on several major sources of energy found on Earth. • Fossil fuels are formed from decayed plants and animals.	• Make observations. • Ask questions. • Learn more.	• Apply the steps of scientific investigation. • Define salient characteristics and provide examples of natural resources. • Understand and articulate the difference between renewable and nonrenewable resources.
7	Renewable Energy Resources	• To engage students in an investigation of renewable vs. nonrenewable energy sources, particularly solar energy.	• Change is everywhere. • Change is related to time. • Change can be natural or manmade. • Change may be random or predictable.	• Sources of energy on Earth include sunlight, water, and wind. • Some natural energy resources are renewable and some are not. • Human activity affects the quality of air, water, and habitats. • Conservation and resource renewal protect the quality and quantity of natural resources. • Humans depend on several major sources of energy found on Earth. • Fossil fuels are formed from decayed plants and animals.	• Make observations. • Ask questions. • Learn more. • Design and conduct experiments. • Create meaning. • Tell others what was found.	• Apply the steps of scientific investigation. • Distinguish between renewable and nonrenewable energy sources. • Identify the advantages and disadvantages of using solar energy.
8	What Is Soil, Anyway?	• To introduce students to soil, its different layers, and its role in supporting and nourishing plants.	• Change is everywhere. • Change is related to time. • Change can be natural or manmade. • Change may be random or predictable.	• Soil provides support and nutrients for plants. • Rock, clay, silt, sand, and humus are components of soil. • Topsoil is the upper soil surface and a natural product of the subsoil and bedrock. • Subsoil and bedrock are layers of soil under the topsoil from which topsoil is formed over a long period of time by the action of water.	• Make observations. • Ask questions. • Learn more.	• Apply the steps of scientific investigation. • Identify different types and layers of soil.
9	Soil, Water, and Plants	• To investigate the porosity of different types of soil. • To evaluate the effectiveness of each type of soil for plants.	• Change is everywhere. • Change is related to time. • Change can be natural or manmade. • Change may be random or predictable.	• Soil provides support and nutrients for plants. • Rock, clay, silt, sand, and humus are components of soil.	• Make observations. • Ask questions. • Learn more. • Design and conduct experiments. • Create meaning. • Tell others what was found.	• Apply the steps of scientific investigation. • Explain the concept of porosity. • Understand the benefits and drawbacks of each soil type.

Table 4, continued

Lesson Number	Title	Instructional Purposes	Change Generalizations	Key Science Concepts	Scientific Investigation Skills and Processes	Assessment "Look Fors" Students should be able to:
10	Soil Erosion	• To conduct an experiment with soil erosion. • To connect the erosion process with the weathering process that breaks down rock to create soil over time. • To discuss the possible drawbacks to erosion and how to prevent it.	• Change is everywhere. • Change is related to time. • Change can be natural or manmade. • Change may be random or predictable.	• Human activity affects the quality of air, water, and habitats. • Topsoil is the upper soil surface and a natural product of the subsoil and bedrock. • Subsoil and bedrock are layers of soil under the topsoil from which topsoil is formed over a long period of time by the action of water. • Over time, weather, water, and living things break down rocks and create soil.	• Make observations. • Ask questions. • Learn more. • Design and conduct experiments. • Create meaning. • Tell others what was found.	• Apply the steps of scientific investigation. • Understand the process of erosion. • Distinguish between natural erosion and manmade erosion.
11	Land Pollution: Garbage!	• To discuss the issue of land pollution (waste disposal). • To investigate the types of waste that students dispose of at school. • To articulate solutions to land pollution problems.	• Change is everywhere. • Change is related to time. • Change can be natural or manmade.	• Human activity affects the quality of air, water, and habitats. • Conservation and resource renewal protect the quality and quantity of natural resources.	• Make observations. • Ask questions. • Learn more.	• Apply the steps of scientific investigation. • Understand the issue of land pollution. • Articulate possible solutions to land pollution.
12	Oil Spill!	• To illustrate the effects of a manmade disaster—an oil spill—on Earth's natural resources. • To make inferences about how an oil spill might affect Queen Anne's Island and about the best method for cleaning up oil spills.	• Change can be natural or manmade. • Change may be random or predictable.	• Sources of energy on Earth include sunlight, water, and wind. • Some natural energy resources are renewable and some are not. • Human activity affects the quality of air, water, and habitats. • Conservation and resource renewal protect the quality and quantity of natural resources.	• Make observations. • Ask questions. • Learn more. • Design and conduct experiments. • Create meaning. • Tell others what was found.	• Apply the steps of scientific investigation. • Identify the causes and effects of water pollution on wildlife and the environment.
13	Planning Preservation Park	• To guide students to begin to connect everything they have learned in this unit to develop a plan for Preservation Park on Queen Anne's Island.	• Change is everywhere. • Change is related to time. • Change can be natural or manmade. • Change may be random or predictable.	• Sources of energy on Earth include sunlight, water, and wind. • Some natural energy resources are renewable and some are not. • Human activity affects the quality of air, water, and habitats. • Conservation and resource renewal protect the quality and quantity of natural resources. • Humans depend on several major sources of energy found on Earth. • Soil provides support and nutrients for plants. • Rock, clay, silt, sand, and humus are components of soil. • Topsoil is the upper soil surface and a natural product of the subsoil and bedrock.	• Make observations. • Create meaning. • Tell others what was found.	• Make connections between lessons on soil, natural resources, and energy sources. • Understand that creativity applies new knowledge to the development of a plan to protect natural resources. • Work collaboratively with others.

Table 4, continued

Lesson Number	Title	Instructional Purposes	Change Generalizations	Key Science Concepts	Scientific Investigation Skills and Processes	Assessment "Look Fors" Students should be able to:
14	Preservation Park Planning Committee	• To help students demonstrate their understanding of the concepts covered in this unit: soil, natural resources, the renewal of natural resources and energy sources, particularly solar energy.	• Change is everywhere. • Change is related to time. • Change can be natural or manmade. • Change may be random or predictable.	• Sources of energy on Earth include sunlight, water, and wind. • Some natural energy resources are renewable and some are not. • Human activity affects the quality of air, water, and habitats. • Conservation and resource renewal protect the quality and quantity of natural resources. • Fossil fuels are formed from decayed plants and animals. • Humans depend on several major sources of energy found on Earth. • Soil provides support and nutrients for plants. • Rock, clay, silt, sand, and humus are components of soil. • Topsoil is the upper soil surface and a natural product of the subsoil and bedrock. • Subsoil refers to the layers of soil under the topsoil from which topsoil is formed over a long period of time by the action of the water. • Over time, weather, water, and living things help break down rocks and create soil.	• Tell others what was found.	• Demonstrate understanding of the key science concepts. • Demonstrate an understanding of the relationship between the planning of Preservation Park and the concept of change. • Articulate ideas clearly and coherently.
15	Wrap It Up!	• To summarize conceptual understanding, key science concepts, and the scientific investigation process.	• Change is everywhere. • Change is related to time. • Change can be natural or manmade. • Change may be random or predictable.	• Sources of energy on Earth include sunlight, water, and wind. • Some natural energy resources are renewable and some are not. • Human activity affects the quality of air, water, and habitats. • Conservation and resource renewal protect the quality and quantity of natural resources. • Humans depend on several major sources of energy found on Earth. • Fossil fuels are formed from decayed plants and animals. • Soil provides support and nutrients for plants. • Rock, clay, silt, sand, and humus are components of soil. • Topsoil is the upper soil surface and a natural product of the subsoil and bedrock. • Subsoil refers to the layers of soil under the topsoil from which topsoil is formed over a long period of time by the action of the water. • Over time, weather, water, and living things help break down rocks and create soil.	• Make observations. • Ask questions. • Learn more. • Design and conduct experiments. • Create meaning. • Tell others what was found.	• Describe how change occurs in natural resources and how humans change the environment. • Draw a concept map for the key science concepts and terms used in the unit. • Describe the scientific investigation process and explain its application to the macroconcept and the key science concepts in the unit.
	Postassessment					

Preteaching Lesson: Science Safety

Planning the Lesson

Instructional Purpose
- To instill in students the importance of safety in the classroom.
- To outline science safety rules to be implemented throughout the unit.

Instructional Time
- 45 minutes

Note to Teacher
Please read Science Safety Guidelines (Handout 0A) prior to teaching this lesson.

Materials/Resources/Equipment
- Sample materials:
  - Soil
  - Plastic bag of nonhazardous powdery substance (e.g., sugar)
  - Closed jar of nonhazardous liquid (e.g., water)

- Plastic disposable gloves
- Safety goggles
- Chart paper
- Markers
- Copies of Handout 0A (Science Safety Guidelines)
- Poster of Handout 0B (Science Safety Rules)

Implementing the Lesson

1. Display sample materials on a long table in front of students. Inform students that they soon will begin a science unit in which they will observe and study many different kinds of materials, such as these. Explain that it is important for students to practice safety during the investigations. Relate the necessity of science safety rules to those of the classroom and physical education.

2. Display and define each item. Tell students that as a class they will create a list of rules they should follow when handling these materials. Have students think of how they can keep their bodies safe. Record these examples on chart paper.

3. Next, unveil the Science Safety Rules (Handout 0B) on chart paper. Have students compare the two lists. How do students' examples relate to these rules? If necessary, add additional rules to the list.

4. Explain why some materials (e.g., knives) or elements (e.g., fire) are never appropriate for children to handle in school. Briefly discuss the potential hazards associated with these.

5. Finally, conduct a brief demonstration to illustrate how to practice safety guidelines. Take the plastic bag containing a nonhazardous powdery substance and the jar of nonhazardous liquid. Explain that you are going to investigate how the two materials interact. Ask students how you can be safe while doing this investigation. Reinforce that substances can be harmful to the eyes or skin and that they should **never** be ingested. Explain that the same is true of soil, which can be toxic to humans. Emphasize that students should follow similar guidelines when studying soil.

6. Following students' examples of safety measures, demonstrate how to use safety goggles to protect the eyes, plastic gloves to protect the hands, and other relevant protective measures, such as pulling long hair back and wearing appropriate clothing. Conduct the demonstration by carefully pouring the powdery substance into the jar of liquid. Emphasize that you should never touch your face or mouth (and especially should not eat or drink) during science experiments.

7. Tell students that materials will be disposed of properly by the teacher after the investigation is completed. Students should not touch any potentially harmful substances.

8. Demonstrate the final rule, "Wash your hands," by properly removing the gloves (without the outside of the gloves ever touching the body) and the goggles. If there is a sink in the classroom, demonstrate how to properly wash one's hands. If no sink is present, inform students that after each investigation the class will go to the bathroom to wash their hands.

9. Conclude the lesson by emphasizing that science investigations are interesting and fun, but they also can be dangerous if not conducted properly. By following the Science Safety Rules, the class will enjoy the benefits of learning about science.

Handout 0A
Science Safety Guidelines

1. Know and follow your school's policies and procedures regarding classroom safety.

2. Always provide direct adult supervision when students are engaging in scientific experimentation.

3. Ensure that all materials and equipment are safe for handling by primary students.

4. Exert extra caution when materials have the potential for harm when used improperly.

5. Use protective gear for eyes, skin, and breathing when conducting experiments, and require students to do the same.

6. Always conduct an experiment by yourself before completing it with the students.

7. Store materials for experiments out of the reach of students.

8. Never allow students to eat or drink during science experiments.

9. Follow general safety rules for sharp objects, heated items, breakables, or spilled liquids.

10. Teach students that it is unsafe to touch their face, mouth, eyes, or other body parts when they are working with plants, animals, microorganisms, or chemicals. Wash hands prior to touching anything. Caution students about putting anything in their mouth or breathing in the smell of substances.

11. Be aware of students' allergies to plants (including plant pollen) animals, foods, chemicals, or other substances to be used in the science classroom. Take all precautions necessary. Common food allergens include peanuts, tree nuts (cashews, almonds, walnuts, hazelnuts, macadamia nuts, pecans, pistachios, and pine nuts), shellfish, fish, milk, eggs, wheat, and soy.

12. Use caution with plants. Never allow students to pick or handle any unknown plants, leaves, flowers, seeds, or berries. Use gloves to touch unknown plants. Many common house, garden, and wooded area plants are toxic.

13. Avoid glass jars and containers. Use plastic, paper, or cloth containers.

14. Thermometers should be filled with alcohol, not mercury.

15. Clearly label any chemicals used and dispose of properly.

16. Teach students safety rules for science (see Handout 0B), including:
    a. **Always** do scientific experiments with an adult present.
    b. **Never** mix things together (liquids, powders) without adult approval.
    c. **Use** your senses carefully. Protect your eyes, ears, nose, mouth, and skin.
    d. **Wash your hands** after using materials for an experiment.

Science Safety Rules

1 **Always** do scientific experiments with an adult present.

2 **Never** mix things together (liquids, powders) without adult approval.

3 **Use** your senses carefully. Protect your eyes, ears, nose, mouth, and skin.

4 **Wash your hands** after using materials for an experiment.

Preassessment Directions
for the Teacher

Planning the Lesson

Instructional Purpose
- To determine prior knowledge of unit content.
- To build understanding of the unit macroconcept, science content, and science processes.

Instructional Time
- Macroconcept assessment: 20 minutes
- Key science concepts assessment: 30 minutes, including preteaching activity
- Scientific process assessment: 20 minutes

Materials/Resources/Equipment
- Copies of preassessments for the unit (Preassessment for Change Concept, Preassessment for Key Science Concepts, and Preassessment for Scientific Process) for each student
- Copies of blank concept map drawing sheet for each student
- Preteaching for Key Science Concepts Preassessment instructions for your use
- Rubrics 1–3 (Scoring Rubric for Change Concept, Scoring Rubric for Key Science Concepts, Scoring Rubric for Scientific Process) for your use
- Copy of Sample Concept Map for your use
- Pencils
- Large chart paper
- Drawing paper for each student

Implementing the Lesson
1. Each assessment should be administered on a different day.
2. Explain to students that the class is beginning a new unit of study. Tell them that they will be completing a preassessment to determine what they already know about the topic. Assure them that the assessment is not for a grade and encourage them to do their best.
3. Collect all of the preassessments. Briefly review each assessment and discuss some of the responses in general, indicating that this unit will provide them with more knowledge and skills than they now have.

Scoring
- Score the preassessments using the rubrics provided. Keep the scores and assessments for diagnostic purposes, to organize groups for various activities during the unit, and to compare pre- and postassessment results.

Name:_____ Date:_____

Preassessment for Change Concept

1. Give as many examples of things that change as you can (up to 10).

_____   _____

_____   _____

_____   _____

_____   _____

_____   _____

2. Draw one example of something that changes, showing before and after the change. Provide as many details as you can.

Before   **After**

3. Identify five ways that a tree could change or be changed.

_____

_____

_____

_____

_____

4. What are three things you can say about *all* change?

All change _____

_____

All change _____

_____

All change _____

_____

Name: _____   Date: _____

Rubric 1
Scoring Rubric for Change Concept

Directions for Use: Score students on their completed preassessments.

		5	4	3	2	1	0
1	**Examples of the Concept**	At least 9–10 appropriate examples are given.	At least 7–8 appropriate examples are given.	At least 5–6 appropriate examples are given.	At least 3 appropriate examples are given.	At least 1–2 appropriate examples are given.	No examples are given.
2	**Drawing of Before-After**	The drawing contains five changed elements depicting a before-after situation.	The drawing contains four changed elements depicting a before-after situation.	The drawing contains three changed elements that depict a before-after situation.	The drawing contains two elements and does not clearly indicate a change relationship.	The drawing contains only one picture element or does not show a before-after relationship.	The drawing contains no elements.
3	**Types of Change**	Five different types of changes are identified.	Four different types of changes are identified.	Three different types of changes are identified.	Two different types of changes are identified.	One different type of change is identified.	No type of change is identified.
4	**Generalizations**	Reflects three appropriate generalizations about change.	Reflects three somewhat appropriate generalizations about change.	Reflects two appropriate generalizations about change.	Reflects one appropriate generalization about change.	Reflects only a statement about change.	No statements or generalizations about change are provided.

Total points possible: 20

Preteaching for Key Science Concepts Preassessment

Directions for the Teacher: Say the following bolded directions to students. Directions for you are not bolded.

Sometimes we know a lot about something even before our teachers teach it in school. Sometimes we don't know very much at all, but we like to learn new things.

For example, what would you think about if someone asked you to tell all you know about how *farms* work? What are some of the words you would use?

(List these on a chart.)

What are some of the things that happen on a farm?

(List these on a chart.)

I am going to show you a way I might tell all I know about how farms work.

(Begin a concept map on a large sheet of paper, using pictures and words, making simple links, and emphasizing these links.)

Make your own concept maps on your drawing paper. This practice activity can be done with a partner.

(Share some of the resulting concept maps, encouraging students to articulate their links.)

Preassessment for
Key Science Concepts

Directions to the Teacher: Read the following paragraph to the students.

Today I would like you to think about all of the things you know about soil. Think about the words you would use and the pictures you could draw to make a concept map. Think about the connections you can make. On your concept map paper, draw in pictures and words all that you know about soil. You will be drawing a concept map, just like the ones you did when we discussed the farm. Today's question is: "Tell me everything you know about soil."

Name: _____

Date: _____

Concept Map
Soil

Name: _____ Date: _____

Rubric 2
Scoring Rubric for Key Science Concepts

Directions for Use: Score students on their completed maps.

	5	4	3	2	1	0
Hierarchical Level Each subordinate concept is more specific and less general than the concept drawn above it. Count the number of levels included in the total map.	Five or more levels are identified.	Four levels are identified.	Three levels are identified.	Two levels are identified.	One level is identified.	No hierarchical levels are identified.
Propositions The linking of two concepts indicating a clear relationship is given. Count the total number of propositions identified on the total map.	Twelve or more propositions are provided.	Ten to twelve propositions are provided.	Seven to nine propositions are provided.	Four to six propositions are provided.	One to three propositions are provided.	No propositions are provided.
Examples A valid example of a concept is provided. Count the total number of examples.	Twelve or more examples are provided.	Ten to twelve examples are provided.	Seven to nine examples are provided.	Four to six examples are provided.	One to three examples are provided.	No examples are provided.

Total points possible: 15

Sample Concept Map

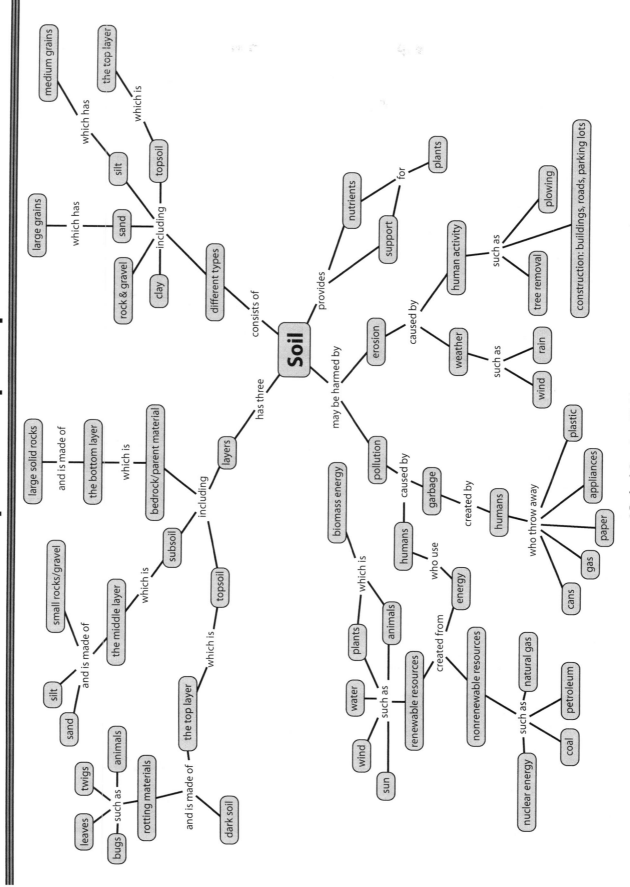

Name:_____ Date:_____

Preassessment for
Scientific Process

Directions: How would you study the question: Are plants attracted to the sun? Describe an experiment to test this question that includes the following:

1. Prediction regarding the question (Are plants attracted to the sun?):

   I predict that_____

   _____

   _____

   _____.

2. What materials will be needed to conduct the experiment?

   _____   _____

   _____   _____

   _____   _____

3. What steps must be taken to conduct the experiment and *in what order?*

   a. _____

   b. _____

   c. _____

   d. _____

   e. _____

4. What data do you want to collect and how should they be recorded?

What will I collect?	How will I record the data?

5. How do the data help me decide if my prediction is correct? Explain.

_____

_____

_____

_____

Name: _____ Date: _____

Rubric 3

Scoring Rubric for Scientific Process

Directions for Use: Score students on the responses to each of the questions.

	Criteria	Strong Evidence 3	Some Evidence 2	Little Evidence 1	No Evidence 0
1	**Generates a Prediction**	Clearly generates a prediction appropriate to the experiment.	Somewhat generates a prediction appropriate to the experiment.	Generates an inappropriate prediction.	Fails to generate a prediction.
2	**Lists Materials Needed**	Provides an inclusive and appropriate list of materials.	Provides a partial list of materials needed.	Provides inappropriate materials.	Fails to provide a list of materials needed.
3	**Lists Experiment's Steps**	Clearly and concisely lists four or more steps as appropriate for the experiment design.	Clearly and concisely lists one to three steps as appropriate for the experiment design.	Generates inappropriate steps.	Fails to generate steps.
4	**Arranges Steps in Sequential Order**	Lists steps in sequential order.	Lists most of the steps or one step out of order.	Lists one or two steps or steps are placed in an illogical order.	Does not list steps.
5	**Plans Data Collection**	Clearly states a plan for data collection, including what data will be needed and how they will be recorded.	States a partial plan for data collection, citing some items for collection and some way of recording data.	Provides a minimal plan for either data collection and/or recording.	Fails to identify any part of a plan for data collection.
6	**States Plan for Interpreting Data for Making Predictions**	Clearly states a plan for interpreting data by linking data to prediction.	States a partial plan for interpreting data that links data to prediction.	Provides a brief statement that partially addresses use of data for prediction.	Fails to state a plan for using data for making a prediction.

Total points possible: 18

Note. Adapted from Fowler (1990).

Lesson 1:
What Is a Scientist?

Planning the Lesson

Instructional Purpose
- To learn the characteristics of scientists and the investigation skills that scientists use.

Instructional Time
- 45 minutes

Scientific Investigation Skills and Processes
- Make observations.
- Ask questions.
- Learn more.
- Design and conduct experiments.
- Create meaning.
- Tell others what was found.

Assessment "Look Fors"
- Students can distinguish between scientists and nonscientists.
- Students should be able to identify the scientific investigation processes used by scientists.

Materials/Resources/Equipment
- Lab coat for teacher
- One lab coat (white adult T-shirt or dress shirt) for each student
- Beaker
- Microscope
- Prepared PowerPoint slides or transparencies of Handout 1A (Completed Frayer Model of Vocabulary Development on Scientists) and Handout 1B (Incomplete Frayer Model of Vocabulary Development on Scientists)
- One copy of Handout 1B (Incomplete Frayer Model of Vocabulary Development on Scientists) for each group of three or four students
- Markers or pens
- One piece of chart paper
- Student log books
- Blank nametags
- *What Is a Scientist?* by Barbara Lehn

Implementing the Lesson

1. Put on a lab coat and pick up a beaker and microscope. Ask the students what kind of job you might have. Explain that you are a scientist. Ask the students if they know a scientist and allow them to discuss what they know about scientists or their experiences with scientists. Record student responses to the following questions:
   - Do you know a scientist?

- What do you think scientists do?
- Name a few famous scientists and discuss their contributions (e. g., Edison—filament).

2. Display the Completed Frayer Model of Vocabulary Development on Scientists (Handout 1A). Cover entries in each section with sticky notes so students cannot read them until the appropriate time. Ask the students what they think scientists do. Write down their definition on the board.
3. Uncover the definition section of the Frayer graphic to reveal the following definition of a scientist: "a person who studies nature and the physical world by testing, experimenting, and measuring" (Scholastic, 1996). Ask students:
   - How is the class' definition of a scientist like (or different from) this definition?

4. Divide the class into small groups of three or four students. Explain and assign roles to each student in the group: recorder, reporter, supporter (manages materials, keeps the group on task, and encourages), and timekeeper.
5. Give each group the incomplete Frayer graphic (Handout 1B) on chart paper with the definition in the appropriate section. Ask groups to write down what a scientist does in the appropriate section (scientific investigation processes). Have reporters share group answers with the class.
6. Using Handout 1A, uncover the section titled "What Scientists Do . . ." to show the science process skills. Ask students to compare and contrast this list with what they wrote down. Quickly explain each item listed and add that students will learn more in the science unit to help them:
   - Make observations.
   - Ask questions.
   - Learn more.
   - Design and conduct experiments.
   - Create meaning.
   - Tell others what was found.

7. Explain that there are many different types of scientists. A geologist is an example of a person who studies the Earth, soil and rock formations, mineral fossils, and natural resources. Have groups write down types of scientists. Share responses with the class and then compare and contrast these responses with the types listed on the large group chart. Note that each word ends with the suffix "-ist" and that this suffix means "a person who."
8. Repeat the process described above for #7 and ask students to give nonexamples of scientists and then share their responses. Lead students in a discussion about whether anyone can be a scientist, using the following prompts:
   - Explain whether you think everyone is a scientist.
   - What makes someone a scientist?
   - When is someone *not* a scientist?

9. Explain to the students that they are going to learn how to think like a scientist and learn how to do what scientists do. Show students the book, *What Is a Scientist?* by Barbara Lehn. Tell students to look for the scientific investigation processes while you are reading the book to them. Refer to the "What Scientists Do . . ." list and discuss the following after reading the book:
   - What scientific investigation skills did we read about in the book?

- What scientific investigation processes do you use? When do you use them?
- What is something you would like to investigate?

10. Have students put on their "lab coats" and nametags with "Professor (child's name)." Tell them to get used to feeling like a scientist because during Lesson 3 they are going to be engaging in the scientific investigation process.

11. Tell students that scientists keep a scientific investigation log of what they are doing. They date the pages in their logs and then write down what they have learned or what they are thinking about what they have learned. Tell students that they are going to keep a log and they are going to make the first page. Distribute one log book to each student. Ask students to date the first page and respond to the prompt, "To think like a scientist means I will . . ." If time allows, have students share their responses.

Concluding and Extending the Lesson

Concluding Questions and/or Actions
- Describe how scientists study change.
- Describe whether you would or would not like to be a scientist.

What to Do at Home
- Tell students to ask their parent or some other adult to respond to the question, "What would you investigate/study/do if you were a scientist?"

Completed Frayer Model of Vocabulary Development on Scientists

Definition	What Scientists Do . . . (Scientific Investigation Processes)
"a person who studies nature and the physical world by testing, experimenting, and measuring"	• Make observations. • Ask questions. • Learn more. • Design and conduct experiments. • Create meaning from experiments. • Tell others what was found.

Scientists

Examples	Nonexamples
• Astronomers—study the universe (planets, stars, etc.) • Biologists—study living plants and animals • Geologists—study the Earth's layers of soil and rocks (sediments and mineral fossils) • Physicists—study matter and energy	• Entertainers • Poets • Bankers

Incomplete Frayer Model of Vocabulary Development on Scientists

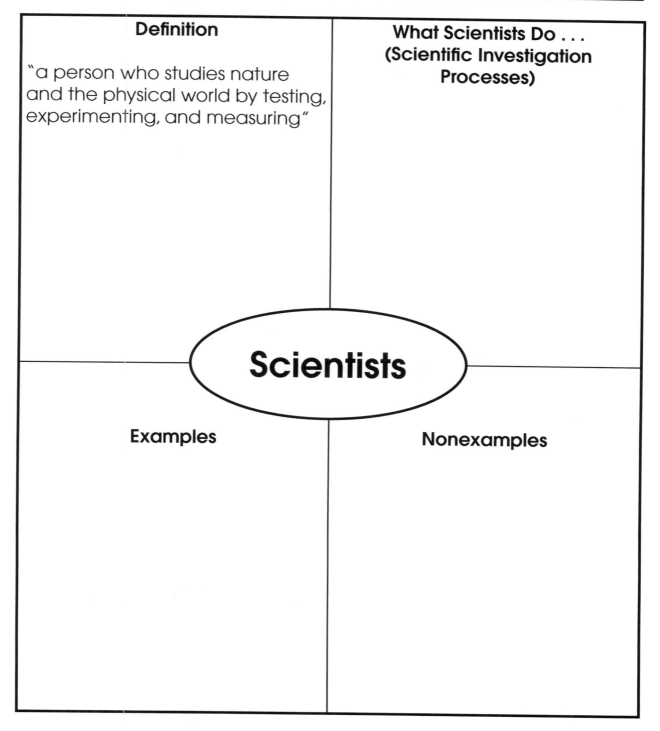

Definition

"a person who studies nature and the physical world by testing, experimenting, and measuring"

**What Scientists Do . . .
(Scientific Investigation Processes)**

Scientists

Examples

Nonexamples

Lesson 2:
What Is Change?

Planning the Lesson

Instructional Purpose
- To develop an understanding of the concept of change.
- To make generalizations about change.

Instructional Time
- 45 minutes

Change Concept Generalizations
- Change is everywhere.
- Change is related to time.
- Change can be natural or manmade.
- Change may be random or predictable.

Scientific Investigation Skills and Processes
- Make observations.

Assessment "Look Fors"
- Students can identify change.
- Students can use the five senses to determine change.
- Students can apply change generalizations appropriately to determine changes.

Materials/Resources/Equipment
- One pack of sticky notes per each group of three to four students
- Chart paper for each group of three to four students, with Handout 2A printed or drawn on it (Taba Concept Model for Change)
- Markers
- A large class poster of Handout 2A
- Four sentence strips with different change generalizations written on each strip
- Strawberry or cherry Kool-Aid®
- Pitcher of water
- Drinking glass (needs to be glass)
- Metal object (e.g., spoon)
- Food coloring

Implementing the Lesson
1. Tell students they are going to explore a concept that is important to understanding our world—change. Explain that scientists spend quite a lot of their time either trying to explain why a change occurred or making changes occur. Ask students how they think scientists study change.
2. Explain that scientists often study change using their senses.
   - Say to the students: "We have five senses; what are they?"
   - Show the students a glass of plain water. Ask students to describe the water only by looking at it: "What do you see?"

- Tell the students to close their eyes. Then add two or three drops of food coloring. Have them open their eyes. Ask: "How did the water change? What sense did you use to determine the change?"
- Show the students a similar glass of plain water filled a quarter full. Strike the glass with a metal object such as a spoon or knife. Ask: "What do you hear?"
- Next tell the students to close their eyes again. Once the students' eyes are closed, fill the glass with more water so that it is half full and strike the glass with the metal object again. Say to the students: "Keep your eyes closed. Did you hear a change in the sound the glass of water made? What kind of change? What do you think I did to the water to change the sound?"
- Tell the students to open their eyes and determine if their predictions were correct. Ask: "What senses did you use to determine the change to the water?"
- Pass around a glass of water and have the students smell the water. Ask: "How does the water smell?"
- Tell the students to close their eyes. When they do, add some strawberry Kool-Aid. Say to the students: "Keep your eyes closed. Smell the water now. Does it smell different? How do you think I changed the water?"
- Tell the students to open their eyes to check the accuracy of their predictions. Ask the students: "How did you know there was a change in the water?"

3. Display the Taba Concept Model for Change (Handout 2A) chart.
4. Create small groups of three or four students each. Give each group sticky notes, markers, and a chart with the Taba Concept Model for Change graphic. Tell each group to think of examples of change and to write or draw one idea per sticky note. Circulate as the groups complete this task, checking for student understanding of the task. Have each group share its examples with the whole class, and write examples from each group on the whole class chart. After each group has shared, have them place their sticky notes on their group's chart section labeled "Examples of Change."
5. Discuss what it means to classify things, modeling the classification of several objects into different categories. Remind students that in order to classify objects, they must find some way in which the objects are similar or alike. Ask groups to classify their sticky notes of change examples into categories. Once the students are satisfied with their categories, have them put them together in a group in the categories box of their chart. Then have them label each category. Have each group share the categories they identified with the whole class, and then write down the categories on the section of the class chart labeled "Categories of Change."
6. In their groups, have students brainstorm nonexamples of change. Ask each student to write one example per sticky note, and have each group share its nonexamples with the whole class. Students should write their nonexamples on their group chart. Then, write the nonexamples on the class chart.
7. Ask the students what they know about change by looking at the examples and nonexamples. Provide the students one statement as a model (e.g., "I notice that there are many different kinds of changes."). Write down your statement on the section of the class chart labeled "Generalizations About Change." Explain that scientists often "generalize" or make statements about what they notice across several examples, observations, or investigations and that these generalizations help scientists to understand our world. In order to

make generalizations, a scientist must infer how the examples, observations, or investigations are alike.

8. Ask each group of students to pretend they are scientists and to come up with one generalization they know about change. Ask them to write that example on the chart section labeled "Generalizations About Change." Circulate as the students work in small groups to facilitate understanding of the word generalization. Ask groups to share their generalizations.

9. Present the following generalizations by pasting sentence strips with generalizations in the section of the class chart labeled "Generalizations About Change" and explain that the students will be looking at how these generalizations help scientists to understand matter:
   - Change is everywhere.
   - Change is related to time.
   - Change can be natural or manmade.
   - Change may be random or predictable.

10. Ask the students to go back to the water examples and tell how the change generalizations apply to the various changes witnessed.

11. Post the chart with generalizations about change in the classroom.

Concluding and Extending the Lesson

Concluding Questions and/or Actions
- How do you think scientists study change?
- Which of your change categories would be helpful to scientists? Why?
- Which are easier to identify: examples or nonexamples of change? Why?
- Why do you think that scientists make generalizations about what they observe or investigate?
- What does a scientist have to do in order to make a generalization?
- Do you think that a generalization is always true? Why or why not?
- What would happen if a scientist found out that a generalization was not true?

What to Do at Home
- Ask students to talk with a family member about a time when a change had a positive effect on the family. Students should come to the next class prepared to share what they learned.

Taba Concept Model for Change

Examples of Change	Categories of Change
Nonexamples of Change	**Generalizations About Change**

Lesson 3:
What Scientists Do

Planning the Lesson

Instructional Purpose
- To introduce the Wheel of Scientific Investigation and Reasoning.
- To apply the scientific investigation process described in the wheel to initiate an investigation of the power of the wind.

Instructional Time
- Part I: 30 minutes
- Part II: 30 minutes

Change Concept Generalizations
- Change is everywhere.
- Change is related to time.
- Change can be natural or manmade.
- Change may be random or predictable.

Key Science Concepts
- Sources of energy on Earth include sunlight, water, and wind.
- Some natural energy sources are renewable and some are not.

Scientific Investigation Skills and Processes
- Make observations.
- Ask questions.
- Learn more.
- Design and conduct experiments.
- Create meaning.
- Tell others what was found.

Assessment "Look Fors"
- Students can apply the steps of the scientific investigation process.
- Students can interpret data from a data table.

Materials/Resources/Equipment
- Lab coat for teacher
- One lab coat for each student
- One feather for each group
- One cardboard tube for each group (i.e., paper towel tube), cut into small rings
- Clear tape for each group
- One length of string for each group (all the same length)
- One small battery-operated fan or hair dryer for each group
- One stopwatch for each group
- Student log books
- Charts or slides of Handouts 3A (Wheel of Scientific Investigation and Reasoning), 3B (Small-Group Observations of Wind Sources), 3C (Wind

Classifications Blank Concept Map), and 3D (Wind Classifications Completed Concept Map)
- Student copies or charts (if using small groups) of Handouts 3A, 3B, and 3C
- Markers or pens for students
- Sentence strip with the question, "Which type of wind energy will move the feather along the strip the fastest?"
- Rulers or yardsticks (optional)

Implementing the Lesson

Part I: Observe, Question, Learn More

1. Have students put on lab coats. Explain to students that they are going to learn to "think like a scientist" and learn how to use the processes of science.
2. Ask students to share their log responses (if not already shared), as well as their parents' responses, to the prompt, "To think like a scientist means I will . . ."
3. Review what a scientist does based on the book *What Is a Scientist?* Tell students they will be learning more about what scientists do.
4. Distribute copies of the Wheel of Scientific Investigation and Reasoning (Handout 3A) to all students and briefly mention its six components. Discuss the following:
   - What do you notice about the Wheel of Scientific Investigation and Reasoning?
   - What processes do you think that scientists use *before* they conduct an experiment?
   - What do scientists do to conduct an experiment?
   - What do scientists do *after* they conduct an experiment?
   - Which part of an investigation do you think would be most difficult? Why?
   - Why do you think the scientific investigation process is on a wheel?

5. Tell students they are going to be scientists today and work through the first three steps of the scientific investigation process. Divide students into groups of three or four, and distribute feathers, tape, string, yardsticks, and fans to each group.
6. Direct students' attention to the first section of the wheel: Make Observations. Complete the following tasks:
   - Explain that scientists record their observations because it helps them to think through a problem and to remember all of the information. Have the students use their log books to write their initial observations about the two types of wind energy. Have a group member create wind with his or her mouth by blowing as if blowing out birthday candles. Ask students: What do you notice about this kind of wind energy?
   - Have students turn on their small fan. Ask students: What do you notice about this kind of wind energy?
   - Students should record their observations in their log books.

7. Explain that sometimes scientists use charts to organize and record their observations. Introduce Handout 3B and model how the students will use the Observation Chart. Complete the following tasks:
   - Have a group member place the feather on a desk and blow the feather with his or her mouth. Ask students: What happens to the feather?

- Have a group member place the feather on a desk and use the fan to blow the feather. Ask students: What happens to the feather?
- Students should record their observations on the chart.

8. Direct students' attention to the second section of the wheel: Ask Questions. Tell students they are going to ask questions about wind and energy. Explain that wind is a form of energy. Ask students:
   - What is energy?
   - What are some sources of energy on Earth?
   - What do you know about the power of the wind?

9. Refer to the third section of the wheel: Learn More. Ask students:
   - What more do you want to learn about the wind?
   - How can you learn more about something?
   - What do you think is the best way to learn more? Why?

Concluding and Extending the Lesson, Part I

What to Do at Home
- Ask students to work with their parents and learn more about wind energy by using books, encyclopedias, the Internet, and so on. Tell them to be prepared to share one fact about wind energy with their classmates.

Part II: Experiment, Create Meaning, Tell Others

1. Review the facts about wind energy that the students found from the previous lesson. Record the facts and encourage students to write them in their log books.
2. Divide students into the same groups as Part I and distribute materials. Tell students they are going to compare the power of two different types of wind. Distribute the cardboard tubes. Tell students to tape a feather to a cardboard tube. Have students thread the cardboard tube onto the string. Have the students tape the string between two desks (or other furniture or structures) so that the string is horizontally suspended and taut, and the cardboard can move easily along the string. Have the students place the yardstick parallel to the string so that they can measure the movement of the cardboard tube along the string. Check the placement of the yardsticks to ensure accuracy in measurement.
3. Tell students to designate the following roles to members of their group:
   - Wind Creator—will create wind by blowing the feather along the string; will measure the distance the feather moves along the yardstick
   - Fan Operator—will create wind by turning on the fan and directing the wind at the feather; will measure the distance the feather moves along the yardstick
   - Timer—will use a stopwatch to time how long it takes for each person to get the tube across the string
   - Recorder—will record the group's observations and the times for each type of wind

4. Point out that another way that scientists learn more is by conducting experiments and making additional observations. Direct students' attention to the fourth section of the wheel: Design and Conduct the Experiment. Model

this section by writing down one question you have on a sentence strip (do ahead of time) such as the following:
- Which type of wind energy will move the feather along the string the fastest?

5. Ask students if they have other questions. Write down their questions on chart paper.
6. Tell students that scientists make predictions and conduct experiments to try to answer their questions. Ask the students to make a prediction about which type of wind energy will move the feather along the string the fastest and write it in their log books. Then, write their predictions on chart paper.
7. Instruct students to "try out" the different types of wind power. Tell students to set up with the Wind Creator holding the feather at one end of the string. When the Timer says "go," the Wind Creator should blow the feather along the string to the end as quickly as he or she can. His or her time should be recorded by the Recorder. If the Wind Creator could not move the feather along the entire length of the string, then the distance should also be measured. The same process should be repeated with the Fan Operator. Ask the students to record the time (and distance) in the Results chart on Handout 3B.
8. Have students answer the following questions in their log books:
- What differences do you observe? What might cause the differences?
- Is one wind type more consistent than the other? Why or why not?
- What other experiments could you conduct to find out more about wind energy using these materials (i.e., distance with a measured number of blows or pulses on the fan)?

9. Ask students to share their findings with the other groups, including:
- Do you think one type of wind would be a better energy source than the other? Why or why not?
- Name one or two things for which each type of wind energy would work well.
- Why do you think _____ was faster than _____?

10. Lead students in creating a concept map on wind classifications. To begin this activity, tell students: "We have just conducted an experiment about wind types. Let's review what we now understand in classifying wind types. I am going to teach you how you can show what you have learned and understand in a way that will help you remember." Show them the slide of Handout 3C or distribute copies of the handout. Tell students: "We know that winds are different due to different characteristics." Use the following questions as a guide for completing the concept map activity. Model on the slide with Handouts 3C and 3D as students work with their own copy. Ask students:
- How did our types of winds vary (e.g., different speeds, different strengths)?
- Why do you think the fan-generated wind was faster than our own wind (e.g., different pressure forces)?

11. Ask students to complete another entry in their log books answering the following prompt and date the page.
- When observing the power of wind, I found that _____ gave me the most helpful information because . . .

Concluding and Extending the Lesson

Concluding Questions and/or Actions

- According to the Wheel of Scientific Investigation and Reasoning, how were you like a scientist?
- What change generalizations can you apply to our investigation?

Handout 3A
Wheel of Scientific Investigation and Reasoning

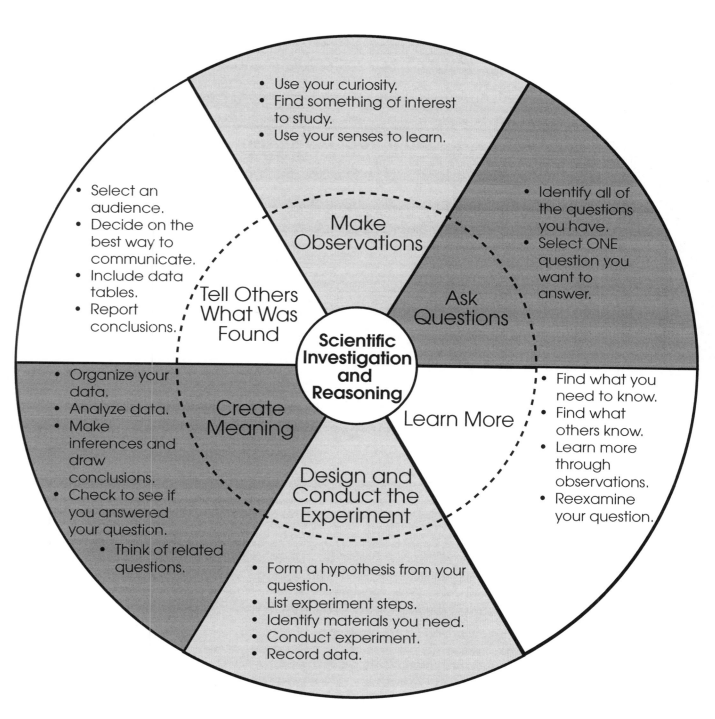

- Use your curiosity.
- Find something of interest to study.
- Use your senses to learn.

- Identify all of the questions you have.
- Select ONE question you want to answer.

- Select an audience.
- Decide on the best way to communicate.
- Include data tables.
- Report conclusions.

Make Observations

Tell Others What Was Found

Ask Questions

Scientific Investigation and Reasoning

- Organize your data.
- Analyze data.
- Make inferences and draw conclusions.
- Check to see if you answered your question.
- Think of related questions.

Create Meaning

Learn More

- Find what you need to know.
- Find what others know.
- Learn more through observations.
- Reexamine your question.

Design and Conduct the Experiment

- Form a hypothesis from your question.
- List experiment steps.
- Identify materials you need.
- Conduct experiment.
- Record data.

Note. Adapted from Kramer (1987).

Name:_____ Date:_____

Small-Group Observations of Wind Sources

Observations

Directions: Describe what happens to the feather when it is blown by each type of wind.

	Mouth-Blown Wind	Fan
Description of feather		

Results

Comparing the Two Types of Wind Energy

	Mouth-Blown Wind	Fan
Time		
Distance (optional)		

Name:_____ Date:_____

Wind Classifications
Blank Concept Map

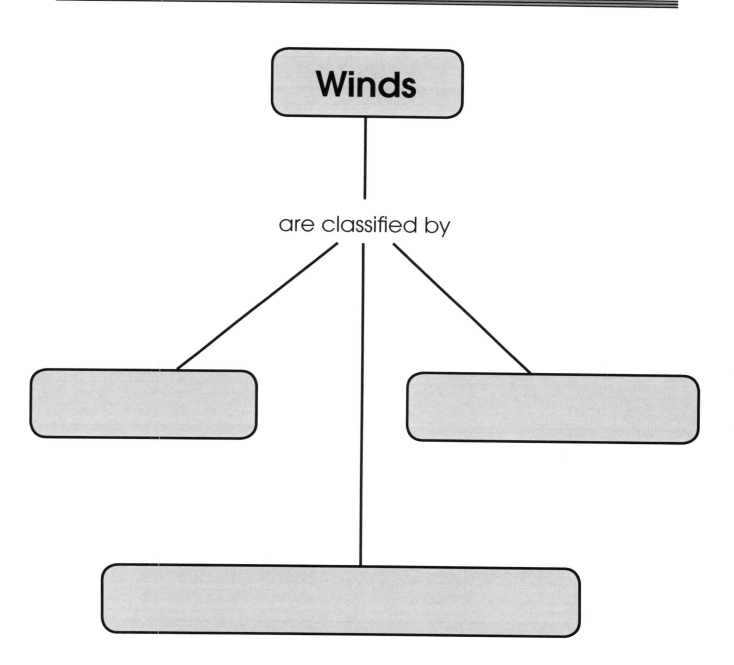

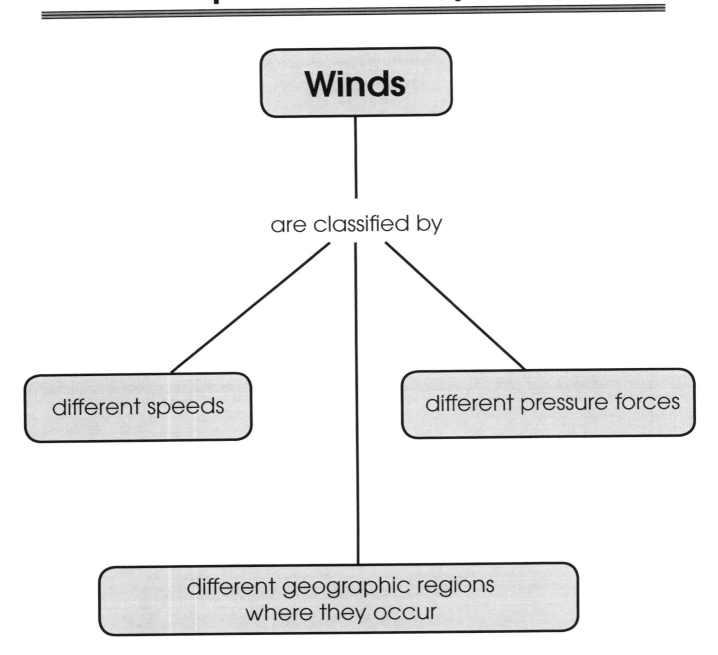

Wind Classifications
Completed Concept Map

Lesson 4:
Preservation Park

Planning the Lesson

Instructional Purpose
- To introduce students to a scenario they will be using throughout the unit to explore change, the key science concepts, and the scientific investigation process.

Instructional Time
- 45 minutes

Change Concept Generalizations
- Change is everywhere.
- Change is related to time.
- Change can be natural or manmade.
- Change may be random or predictable.

Key Science Concepts
- Sources of energy on Earth include sunlight, water, and wind.
- Some natural energy resources are renewable and some are not.
- Human activity affects the quality of air, water, and habitat.
- Conservation and resource renewal protect the quality and quantity of natural resources.
- Humans depend on several major sources of energy found on Earth.

Scientific Investigation Skills and Processes
- Ask questions.
- Learn more.

Assessment "Look Fors"
- Students can apply change generalizations to our environment.
- Students can draw inferences about environmental devastation and pollution.

Materials/Resources/Equipment
- *Common Ground: The Water, Earth, and Air We Share* by Molly Bang
- Handout 4A (Message From Geologist #1), recorded on tape
- Slide of Handout 4B (Need to Know Board)
- Chart paper
- Markers
- Handout 3D, for reference

Implementing the Lesson

1. Recall what a geologist is. Introduce the challenge by saying, "You and your teammates are environmental scientists who have been called into action. Listen to the exciting call that arrived today from a local geologist, then grab

> **Note to Teacher:**
> To add mystery and interest, record the phone message from the geologist while playing the *Mission Impossible* theme song in the background. The theme music can be found by doing a Google search for the music.

your research bags—you are on your way!" Allow students to listen to the phone message left for your team (Handout 4A).

Note to Teacher: Change the time in the phone message to accurately represent the time you anticipate spending on this unit.

2. Display the Need to Know Board (Handout 4B) and record what students know about the problem, what they need to know, and how they can find out. Focus student discussion by asking:
   - What do you think are some problems or issues that might be affecting the environment of Queen Anne's Island?

   Model examples aloud and have students explain why the information is important. Continue the discussion of environmental issues and conservation by encouraging students to talk about how humans can impact wildlife and the environment and how they can combat negative effects on the environment.

3. After students have completed the Need to Know Board, read aloud *Common Ground: The Water, Earth, and Air We Share* by Molly Bang. Ask students:
   - What changes can you identify? Look at our change generalizations. What generalizations apply to what has happened to our Earth?
   - What are the causes of environmental pollution? What kinds of human activity threaten humans, wildlife, and the environment as exhibited in the book?
   - Is there anything we can add to our Need to Know Board? Explain.

4. Divide students into pairs or small groups. Ask them to imagine what might be happening on the island, identifying possible ways to design a preservation garden. Provide groups with large chart paper and markers to record their ideas using the method of their choosing (e.g., lists, drawings). After students have worked for about 10 minutes, allow them to share their ideas and display the charts on the wall. Then, as a class, have students determine the five most commonly held ideas about the solution for the problem on Queen Anne's Island.

Concluding and Extending the Lesson

Concluding Questions and/or Actions
- What is the purpose of conducting this investigation?
- Identify what is changing and what can be changed.
- Based on the description, what do you infer are the central causes of environmental devastation and pollution on Queen Anne's Island?
- How can we learn more about the situation?
- How could one's occupation or beliefs impact his or her decision to become involved in conservation?
- What groups are affected by this investigation?
- Which concept generalizations of cause and effect apply to our investigation?
- How could the scenario relate to your community? What are the central causes of environmental devastation and pollution where you live?
- Ask students to list several concept words they have used in today's lesson. Record these words on chart paper and challenge students to create a connection between two of the words to show their understanding of the concepts. Show the students how to record these as a link that would be part of a concept map. Ask students to complete several connections on

their paper or in their log books. Refer students to Handout 3D if they need examples of connections.

Student Log Book Prompt
- Write about a type of Earth, air, or water pollution you have seen personally. Identify its possible causes and effects.

What to Do at Home
- Have students analyze their hometown and answer the following prompt: Do you think your hometown may have similar environmental concerns as Queen Anne's Island? Why or why not?

Message From Geologist #1

Team, you are needed right away! Queen Anne's Island, located off the Virginia shore, is in an environmental crisis. Many of its water sources have become polluted from industry and traffic. Its farmland has eroded and the air has become increasingly dangerous to breathe. We need your help to assist Queen Anne's Island in designing a park—called Preservation Park—to preserve its natural resources. You have 3 weeks to learn all you can about natural resources, soil, and conservation. Get busy right away!

Name:_____ Date:_____

Handout 4B
Need to Know Board

What Do We Know?	What Do We Need to Know?	How Can We Find Out?

What Have We Learned?

Lesson 5:
Natural Resources, Part I

Planning the Lesson

Instructional Purpose
- To introduce students to the concept of natural resources.
- To explore the interrelationship between living creatures and the environment.

Instructional Time
- 45 minutes

Change Concept Generalizations
- Change is everywhere.
- Change is related to time.
- Change can be natural or manmade.
- Change may be random or predictable.

Key Science Concepts
- Sources of energy on Earth include sunlight, water, and wind.
- Some natural energy resources are renewable and some are not.
- Conservation and resource renewal protect the quality and quantity of natural resources.
- Humans depend on several major sources of energy found on Earth.
- Fossil fuels are formed from decayed plants and animals.

Scientific Investigation Skills and Processes
- Make observations.
- Ask questions.
- Learn more.

Assessment "Look Fors"
- Students can apply the steps of the scientific investigation process.
- Students can define salient characteristics and provide examples of natural resources.
- Students can understand and articulate the difference between renewable and nonrenewable resources.

Materials/Resources/Equipment
- *Brother Eagle, Sister Sky* by Susan Jeffers, or *A Drop Around the World* by Barbara McKinney
- Slide of Handout 5A (Concept Definition Map)
- Slide of Handout 5B (Need to Know Board: Natural Resources)
- Copies of Handouts 5A and 5B, one per group
- Student log books
- Word for word wall: natural resources

Implementing the Lesson

1. Introduce the lesson by selecting and reading one of the following two children's books:
   - Jeffers, S. (2002). *Brother eagle, sister sky.* New York: Puffin.
   - McKinney, B. (1998). *A drop around the world.* Nevada City, CA: Dawn Publications.

   Then, ask students to list what they know about natural resources.

2. Following about 5 minutes of discussion, break students into groups of three or four students. Give each group a Concept Definition Map (Handout 5A). Direct students' attention to the words "Natural Resources" near the middle of the chart. In groups, have students answer the following questions in order:
   - What are natural resources?
   - What are some examples of natural resources?
   - What are the uses of each of those examples?

3. After the groups have completed the chart, allow each group to share some of its ideas. Record the ideas on the overall class chart on the slide or chart paper. Use the ideas from the whole class to develop a class definition of natural resources to include on the word wall. (A sample definition might be "naturally occurring materials that can be used by living things to meet specific needs.") Compare the class definition to the one in the Unit Glossary.

4. Inform students that they must learn more about natural resources in order to design Preservation Park for Queen Anne's Island in future lessons.

5. Assign a natural resource of your choice to each group of students. Make sure to choose natural resources about which it will be relatively easy for students to find information (e.g., fossil fuels, solar energy, wind, soil, water).

6. Give each group a copy of the Need to Know Board: Natural Resources (Handout 5B). Have students complete the board about their assigned natural resource. Students should discuss the following questions within their groups:
   - What should we do first? What next?
   - What questions will we investigate?
   - Who will be assigned to each question?
   - What resources will we use?
   - What is our plan of action?

Concluding and Extending the Lesson

Concluding Questions and/or Actions
- Students can answer the following questions in discussion format or as journal entries in their log books:
  - Why is it important to understand more about our natural resources?
  - Why do you think it is important to know if a natural resource is renewable or nonrenewable?
  - What generalizations about change apply to natural resources?

What to Do at Home
- Ask students to identify items in their homes that are derived from natural resources. Ask them which natural resources they use the most and how they are useful to them. Tell students to be prepared to share their answers with their classmates.

Name:_____ Date:_____

Concept Definition Map

```
┌─────────────────────────────────────┐
│      What Are They? (definition)     │
│                                      │
│                                      │
│                                      │
└─────────────────────────────────────┘
                  ⬆

          ┌───────────────────┐
          │ NATURAL           │
          │ RESOURCES         │
          └───────────────────┘
                  ⬇
```

Example	Example	Example
⬇ Uses	⬇ Uses	⬇ Uses

Name:_____ Date:_____

Need to Know Board: Natural Resources

Our natural resource is _____

What Do We Know?	What Do We Need to Know?	How Can We Find Out?

What Have We Learned?

Lesson 6:
Natural Resources, Part II

Planning the Lesson

Instructional Purpose
- To continue the introduction of students to the concept of natural resources.
- To explore the interrelationship between living creatures and the environment.

Instructional Time
- 45 minutes

Change Concept Generalizations
- Change is everywhere.
- Change is related to time.
- Change can be natural or manmade.
- Change may be random or predictable.

Key Science Concepts
- Sources of energy on Earth include sunlight, water, and wind.
- Some natural energy resources are renewable and some are not.
- Conservation and resource renewal protect the quality and quantity of natural resources.
- Humans depend on several major sources of energy found on Earth.
- Fossil fuels are formed from decayed plants and animals.

Scientific Investigation Skills and Processes
- Make observations.
- Ask questions.
- Learn more.

Assessment "Look Fors"
- Students can apply the steps of the scientific investigation process.
- Students can define salient characteristics and provide examples of natural resources.
- Students can understand and articulate the difference between renewable and nonrenewable resources.

Materials/Resources/Equipment
- *Agatha's Feather Bed: Not Just Another Wild Goose Story* by Carmen Agra Deedy
- Slide of Handout 5A (Concept Definition Map), one copy per group
- Slide of Handout 5B (Need to Know Board: Natural Resources), one copy per group
- Poster board, one piece per group
- Markers, colored pencils, and other art supplies
- Resources for student research (e.g., textbooks, library books, Internet access, articles) on natural resources
- Chart paper or slide of Handout 6A (Renewable vs. Nonrenewable T-Chart)

> **Note to Teacher:**
> Ask the school librarian to help you organize resources for this lesson.

- Student log books
- Copies of Handout 6B (Natural Resources Blank Concept Map) for each student
- Handout 6C (Natural Resources Completed Concept Map)
- United Streaming video clip: *Natural Resources* (11 minutes; optional)

Note to Teacher: Your school may have a subscription to Discovery's United Streaming. If not, visit http://www.unitedstreaming.com to sign up for a free 30-day trial.

Implementing the Lesson

1. Begin the second natural resources lesson by reminding students of the previous class discussion about natural resources (Lesson 5). Illustrate how natural resources are important in everyday life by reading aloud *Agatha's Feather Bed: Not Just Another Wild Goose Story* by Carmen Agra Deedy (1994). During the reading, students should note examples and sources of natural resources (e.g., trees, plants, fossil fuels, silk, sea salt, diamonds, sand) in their log books. Emphasize the book's message:

   Everything comes from something,
   Nothing comes from nothing,
   Just like paper comes from trees,
   And glass comes from sand,
   An answer comes from a question.
   All you have to do is ask.

2. Ask students to get out their Need to Know Boards: Natural Resources (Handout 5B). Allow groups to reconvene and, once students have determined what they need to know, allow each group to access the different materials you've provided about natural resources to complete their boards. Or, show the United Streaming clip, *Natural Resources,* and instruct students to take notes on their group's assigned natural resource.

3. Instruct students to use the poster board and art supplies to create a poster about their natural resource. Tell them to make sure they include information about what the natural resource is and what it is used for.

4. Before students present their posters, share the definitions of "renewable" and "nonrenewable." After each group shares its poster, ask the students if they think their resource is renewable or nonrenewable. Write their answers on the chart or slide of the Renewable vs. Nonrenewable T-Chart (Handout 6A). After listing resources on the T-chart, pass out the Natural Resources Concept Map (Handout 6B). Talk with students about how a concept map also could organize this information. Help the students fill out their concept maps based on what they have learned. (Handout 6C shows an example of a completed concept map; students will do an independent concept map later in the unit.)

5. Tell students they will be learning more about renewable and nonrenewable resources in the next lesson.

Concluding and Extending the Lesson

Concluding Questions and/or Actions

- Students can answer the following questions in discussion format or as journal entries in their log books:

- Which, if any, of the change generalizations apply to what you have learned about the depletion of natural resources?
- How do you think the depletion of natural resources will affect people, wildlife, and the environment?

What to Do at Home

- Ask students to identify items in their homes that are derived from natural resources that can be recycled. Have them identify in what ways they can be recycled. Tell students to be prepared to share their answers with their classmates.

Name:_____ Date:_____

Renewable vs. Nonrenewable T-Chart

Renewable	Nonrenewable

Name:_____ Date:_____

Natural Resources Blank Concept Map

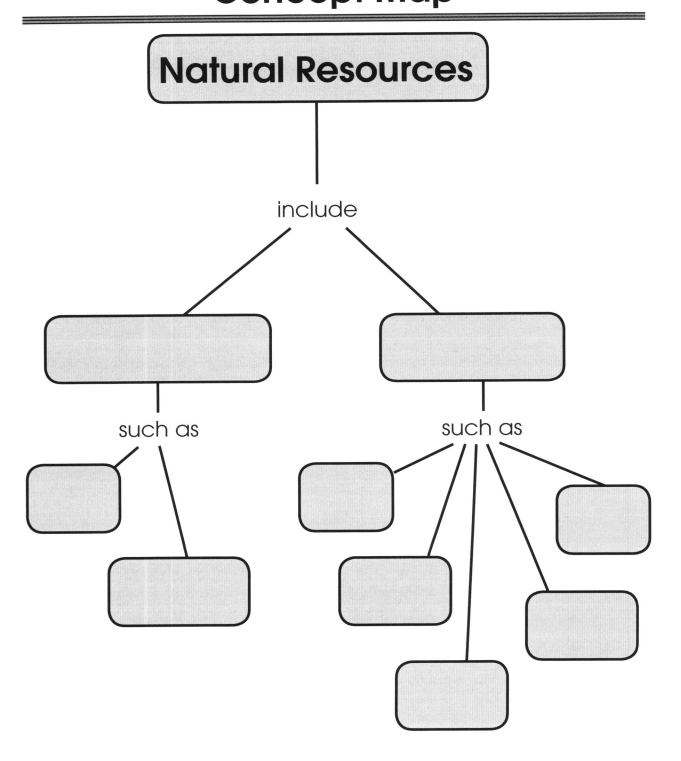

Natural Resources

include

such as

such as

Name:_____ Date:_____

Natural Resources Completed Concept Map

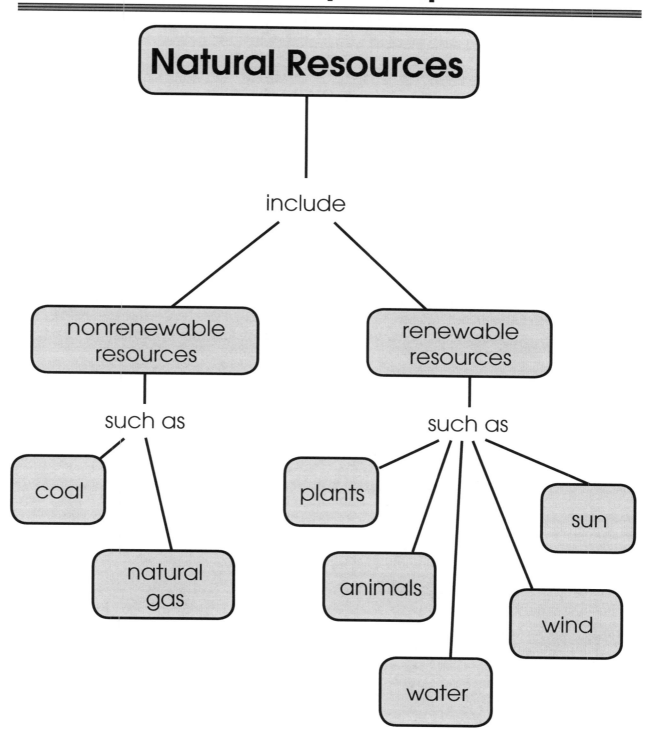

Natural Resources

include

nonrenewable resources

renewable resources

such as

such as

coal

natural gas

plants

animals

water

wind

sun

Lesson 7:
Renewable Energy Resources

Planning the Lesson

Instructional Purpose
- To engage students in an investigation of renewable vs. nonrenewable energy sources, particularly solar energy.

Instructional Time
- 45 minutes

Change Concept Generalizations
- Change is everywhere.
- Change is related to time.
- Change can be natural or manmade.
- Change may be random or predictable.

Key Science Concepts
- Sources of energy on Earth include sunlight, water, and wind.
- Some natural energy resources are renewable and some are not.
- Human activity affects the quality of air, water, land, and habitats.
- Conservation and resource renewal protect the quality and quantity of natural resources.
- Humans depend on several major sources of energy found on Earth.
- Fossil fuels are formed from decayed plants and animals.

Scientific Investigation Skills and Processes
- Make observations.
- Ask questions.
- Learn more.
- Design and conduct experiments.
- Create meaning.
- Tell others what was found.

Assessment "Look Fors"
- Students can apply the steps of the scientific investigation process.
- Students can distinguish between renewable and nonrenewable energy sources.
- Students can identify the advantages and disadvantages of using solar energy.

Materials/Resources/Equipment
- Slide or chart of Handout 7A (Energy Sources: Advantages and Disadvantages)
- Slide or chart of Handout 3A (Wheel of Scientific Investigation and Reasoning)
- Bottles painted white and black, one each per group
- Small latex balloons of the same size and color, one balloon per bottle (*Note:* The balloons can be any color, but you need to use the same color balloon on both bottles to control this variable.)
- A sunny day or a lamp to substitute for the sun (*Note:* Be advised that this experiment works better with actual sunlight.)

- Student log books
- Words for word wall: renewable energy, nonrenewable energy, solar energy
- *My Light* by Molly Bang (optional)
- United Streaming video clip: *The Magic School Bus: Getting Energized* (22 minutes; optional).

Implementing the Lesson

1. Introduce the lesson by asking, "What is an energy source?" Encourage students to think about what they have learned about natural resources. Allow students to brainstorm while recording their ideas on the board or on chart paper.

2. Remind students about the question in Lesson 5 about renewable and nonrenewable resources. Reinforce that renewable energy derives from sources that cannot be "used up," such as sunshine, water flow, wind, and vegetation. Nonrenewable energy sources are those derived from depleted fuels such as oil and gas or from resources like coal that are created over long periods of time through lengthy geological processes and exist in limited quantities. Post the words renewable energy and nonrenewable energy on the word wall.

> **Note to Teacher:**
> If you like, you can introduce this experiment a day early and ask students to wear white or black shirts to school depending on their hypothesis.

3. As a class, come up with a list of three renewable and three nonrenewable energy sources. Write them on the slide or chart of Handout 7A (Energy Sources: Advantages and Disadvantages). Discuss with students the advantages and disadvantages of each of the energy sources listed. In your discussion, consider availability, effects on the environment, practicality, and cost.

4. Ask students to think about which energy source they think is least harmful to the environment and easiest to obtain. Students should determine that solar energy is the most versatile renewable energy source because it is available to everyone everywhere and is nearly inexhaustible.

5. Tell students they are going to conduct an experiment to demonstrate the power of the sun. They are going to answer the question, "Which color best absorbs and stores the sun's energy, white or black?"

6. Direct students' attention to the slide of the Wheel of Scientific Investigation and Reasoning (Handout 3A). Tell students they have already engaged in steps 1 through 3 in an earlier lesson (Lesson 3). They are now on the fourth step.

7. Ask students to record their hypothesis in their student log books by completing the sentence, "I think the color _____ will best absorb the sun's energy."

8. Divide students into groups of three or four. Give each group a black bottle, a white bottle, and two balloons.

9. Tell students to put the balloons over the tops of the bottles, so that the balloon opening is snug over the opening of the bottle. Have each group take its bottle outside and place it in the sun. Tell students to record their observations in their log books after 5 minutes, 10 minutes, and so on. Allow students to stay outside until the balloon on the black bottle has expanded. Encourage students to touch the balloons on each bottle to feel the relative heat of each.

10. Bring students back into the classroom. Direct their attention to the fifth step on the wheel: Create Meaning. Ask students:
    * Why do you think the balloon expanded on the black bottle but not on the white bottle?

    Explain to students that as the black bottle absorbed the sun's energy the air particles inside the bottle were warmed up, which caused them to bounce around faster. The faster movement of air caused the balloon to expand. Because the white bottle didn't absorb the sun's energy, the air didn't move faster, and the balloon didn't expand.
11. Direct students' attention to step 6 on the wheel: Tell Others What Was Found. Ask students how they might share the information they have learned about solar energy with others; encourage them to share their new knowledge with others.
12. Show the video *The Magic School Bus: Getting Energized,* which teaches students about alternative power sources (optional).
13. Read the book *My Light* by Molly Bang. Talk about the book's message about the power of the sun (optional).

Concluding and Extending the Lesson

Concluding Questions and/or Actions
* Why is it important to analyze the advantages and disadvantages of using different energy sources?
* What central problems exist when using renewable energy sources? Nonrenewable energy sources?
* What data or evidence can a scientist gather on the effectiveness of different types of energy sources?
* What did you assume you knew about solar energy prior to this investigation?
* What do you infer about the advantages and disadvantages of using solar energy?
* What are the implications of humans' use of energy sources for the future?
* What generalizations about change apply to renewable energy sources?

Extending the Lesson
* Introduce the modified "Four Corners Debate Strategy," informing students that this debate model will allow them to take a position on solar energy and use research to defend their positions. Place four posters around the classroom labeled "Strongly Agree," "Agree," "Disagree," and "Strongly Disagree." Then give students a few moments to determine their position on the following prompt (to be written on the board): Queen Anne's Island should rely on solar energy instead of fossil fuels for its primary energy source.
* Have students stand in front of the sign that best describes how they feel about this issue. Students will be given a few minutes to discuss why they chose that position in their respective groups (formed based on like responses). Groups will then select one member to record the reasons for the group's position. Each group will be given 2 minutes to present its reasons to the other groups.
* Next, remove the "Strongly Agree" and "Strongly Disagree" posters. Ask students to determine their position based on the information that was presented by each group. Give students a few moments to determine their position on the prompt. Have students stand in front of the sign that best

describes how they feel about this issue, "Agree" or "Disagree." Allow students to switch groups if they were convinced by another group.

- After students move, allow the groups to discuss their reasoning again, this time writing a paragraph to state their position, beginning with "We agree/disagree that Queen Anne's Island should rely on solar energy instead of fossil fuels because. . . ." Each group will be given 3 to 5 minutes to present their argument. The opposing side will be given 1 to 2 minutes to rebut. Following the debate, ask the whole class to determine which arguments were more effective, and why.

What to Do at Home

- Have students identify ways in which their family could use solar energy at home. What are the advantages and disadvantages of using this energy source at home?

Energy Sources: Advantages and Disadvantages

Renewable Energy Source	Advantages	Disadvantages

Nonrenewable Energy Source	Advantages	Disadvantages

Lesson 8:
What Is Soil, Anyway?

Planning the Lesson

Instructional Purpose
- To introduce students to soil, its different layers, and its role in supporting and nourishing plants.

Instructional Time
- 45 minutes

Change Concept Generalization
- Change is everywhere.
- Change is related to time.
- Change can be natural or manmade.
- Change may be random or predictable.

Key Science Concepts
- Soil provides support and nutrients for plants.
- Rock, clay, silt, sand, and humus are components of soil.
- Topsoil is the upper soil surface and a natural product of the subsoil and bedrock.
- Subsoil and bedrock are layers of soil under the topsoil from which topsoil is formed over a long period of time by the action of water.

Scientific Investigation Skills and Processes
- Make observations.
- Ask questions.
- Learn more.

Assessment "Look Fors"
- Students can apply the steps of the scientific investigation process.
- Students can identify the different types and layers of soil.

Materials/Resources/Equipment
- One small bag per group, labeled Samples A, B, C, D, and E, respectively, of the following:
  - Sand
  - Clay (can use modeling clay as substitute if necessary)
  - Silt (can use chalk dust as substitute if necessary)
  - Rocks and gravel
  - Topsoil (potting soil)

- Wide-mouth jar (e.g., pickle jar, large mayonnaise jar) or small fish bowl, one per group
- Magnifying glasses
- Copies of Handout 8A (Characteristics of Soil), one per student or group
- Copies of Handout 8B (Definitions of Soil Types), one per student or group
- Copies of Handout 8C (Layers of Soil), one per student or group

- Copies of Handout 8D (Soil Layers Blank Concept Map), one per student or group
- Copies of Handout 8E (Soil Layers Completed Concept Map), one per student or group
- Student log books

Implementing the Lesson

1. Remind students about the message from the geologist from the earlier lesson. Ask students if they remember what the geologist told them to study. Guide students to the directive from the geologist to learn about soil.
2. Tell students that today they are going to learn about the different layers and types of soil. With the class, define related terms that are important for understanding soils: organisms, weathering, sediments, parent material, time.
3. Divide students into groups of three or four. Give each group a labeled bag of sand, clay, silt, rocks and gravel, and topsoil (potting soil). The bags should be labeled A–E.
4. Give students Handout 8A (Characteristics of Soil).
5. Instruct students to use their senses of sight, smell, and touch to determine the characteristics of each sample. They also can use aids such as magnifying glasses. Tell them to record their observations in the appropriate section of the Characteristics of Soil chart.
6. Once all groups have recorded their observations, give them Handout 8B (Definitions of Soil Type). Using these definitions and their observations, instruct students to identify each type of soil.
7. Allow students to share their answers with the whole class. As a class, make sure each group has identified Sample A as sand, Sample B as clay, Sample C as silt, Sample D as rocks and gravel, and Sample E as topsoil.
8. Tell students that all of the items they have studied are different components of soil.
9. Give students Handout 8C (Layers of Soil) and a jar (or small fish bowl). Tell students they are going to use their samples and observations to create a model of the different layers of soil.
10. Using what they have learned about the different components, tell students to follow the Layers of Soil chart to create their model. They should construct their model as follows from bottom to top:
    - Larger rocks
    - Mixture of small rocks (gravel), clay, sand, and silt
    - Potting soil

11. If time permits, allow students to share their models.
12. Lead students in creating a concept map on soil classifications. (See the Concept Mapping section in Appendix B as a guide for instructing students in concept mapping.) To begin this activity, tell students: "Let's review what we now understand about soil and illustrate our understanding with a concept map." Show them the slide of Handout 8D (Soil Layers Blank Concept Map) or distribute copies of Handout 8D. (Handout 8E shows an example of a completed concept map.) Use the following questions as a guide for completing the concept map activity. Model on the slide with the handouts as students work with their own copy. Ask students:
    - What do we know about soil? (Answer: It is comprised of three layers.)
    - What are the three different layers of soil?
    - What makes each layer different?

Concluding and Extending the Lesson

Concluding Questions and/or Actions
- What are the different layers of soil? Why do you think they are in this order? (Tell students that weather and other natural processes like running rivers break down the rock over time into smaller and smaller pieces.)
- Why do you think it is important for scientists to study soil?

Log Prompt
Students should answer the following in their log books:
- I think soil is important because . . .

What to Do at Home
- After getting permission and determining how deep to dig, have students dig a hole in the soil near where they live. Have them identify the different layers and different components of soil and share their observations with their parents and/or siblings.

Name:_____ Date:_____

Characteristics of Soil

	Sight	Smell	Touch
Sample A			
Sample B			
Sample C			
Sample D			
Sample E			

Name:_____ Date:_____

Definitions of Soil Types

Clay: The type of soil with the smallest grains. You would need a magnifying glass to see the grains of clay. It feels slippery or sticky and breaks into hard clumps if you squeeze it.

Topsoil: The top layer of soil. Topsoil is usually dark brown or black in color. It contains small bits of rotting material such as leaves, twigs, and living and dead organisms. Topsoil feels soft when you rub it between your fingers and slightly spongy if you squeeze it.

Silt: The type of soil with medium-sized grains. Silt feels smooth and silky to the touch.

Sand: The type of soil with the largest grains. Sand feels gritty and easily falls through your fingers. When squeezed, sand falls apart.

Rock and gravel: Solid and hard. These elements are usually brown or gray in color. Sometimes they may have reflective specks that shimmer in the light.

Name:_____ Date:_____

Layers of Soil

Topsoil
- Top layer of soil.
- Usually very dark brown in color.
- Feels soft and spongy to the touch.
- Contains rotting material such as leaves, twigs, and/or insects and animals both living and dead.
- Usually loosely packed.

Subsoil
- Middle layer of soil.
- A mixture of nearly all soil elements.
- It contains a mixture of clay, sand, silt, and small rocks and/or rock pieces.
- Usually tightly packed.

Sediment/Bedrock
- Bottom layer of soil.
- Large, solid rocks.

Name:_____ Date:_____

Soil Layers Blank Concept Map

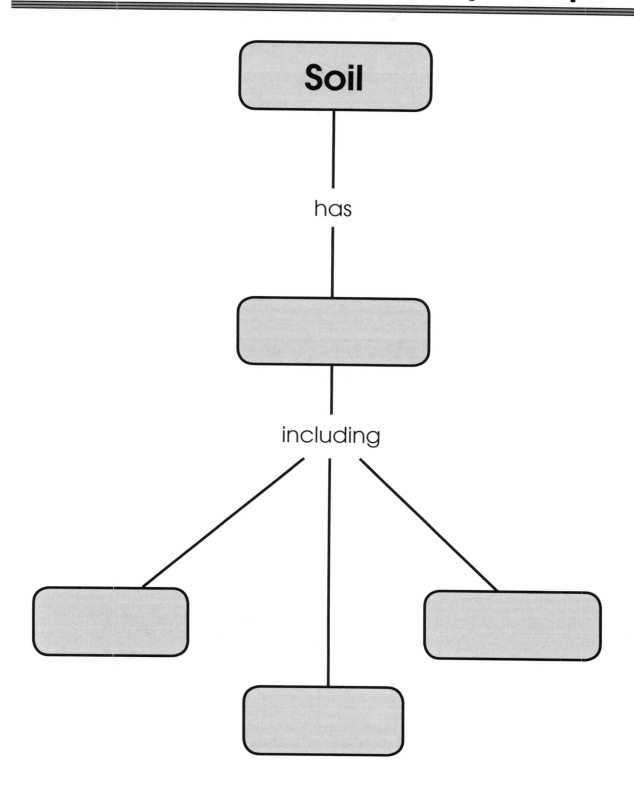

Name:_____ Date:_____

Soil Layers Completed
Concept Map

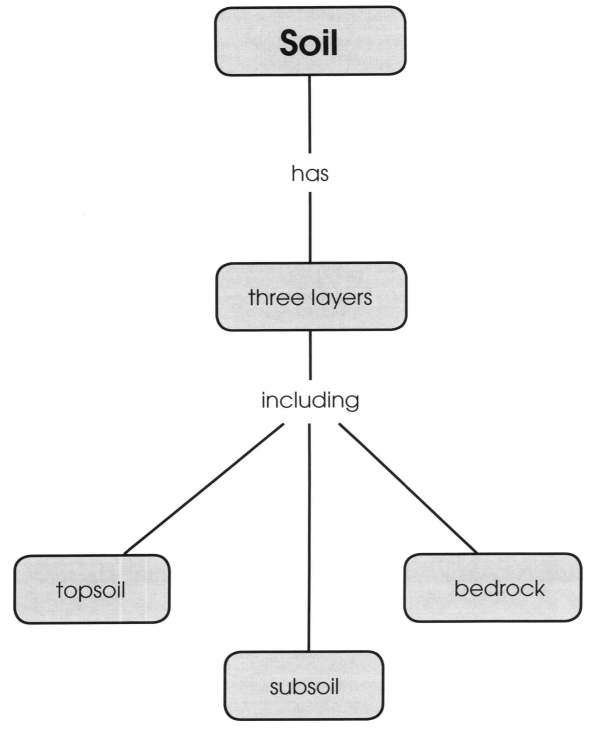

Lesson 9:
Soil, Water, and Plants

Planning the Lesson

Instructional Purpose
- To investigate the porosity of different types of soil.
- To evaluate the effectiveness of each type of soil for plants.

Instructional Time
- 45 minutes

Change Concept Generalizations
- Change is everywhere.
- Change is related to time.
- Change can be natural or manmade.
- Change may be random or predictable.

Key Science Concepts
- Soil provides support and nutrients for plants.
- Rock, clay, silt, sand, and humus are components of soil.

Scientific Investigation Skills and Processes
- Make observations.
- Ask questions.
- Learn more.
- Design and conduct experiments.
- Create meaning.
- Tell others what was found.

Assessment "Look Fors"
- Students can apply the steps of the scientific investigation process.
- Students can explain the concept of porosity.
- Students can understand the benefits and drawbacks of each soil type.

Materials/Resources/Equipment
- One sample of rocks/gravel, clay, sand, and topsoil (potting soil) per group
- Four wide-mouth jars per group
- Filter paper
- Pitcher of water, one per group
- Graduated beaker or measuring cup, one per group
- Potted plant (for demonstration)
- Large jar (for demonstration—should be large enough for the class to see when it is in the front of the room)
- Small spade
- Slide of Handout 3A (Wheel of Scientific Investigation and Reasoning)
- Slide of Handout 9A (Soil Types Blank Concept Map)
- Slide of Handout 9B (Soil Types Completed Concept Map)
- Copies of Handouts 9A and 9B, one per student

- Student log books
- Word for word wall: humus

Implementing the Lesson

1. Display the slide of the Wheel of Scientific Investigation and Reasoning (Handout 3A). Tell students they are going to act like scientists and decide what kind of soil would be best for plants.

2. Divide students into groups of three or four. Ask them to open their log books to a new page and date it. Give each group its samples of rocks/gravel, clay, sand, and topsoil (potting soil). Direct the students' attention to the first step on the wheel: Make observations. Ask them to record their observations about the soil samples in their log books.

3. Direct students' attention to the second step on the wheel: Ask questions. Ask each group to generate questions it might ask about the soil samples. Allow each group to share several of its questions.

4. Direct students' attention to the third step on the wheel: Learn More. Discuss ways in which the students' questions might be answered. When possible, answer their questions using information gained from the previous lesson (Lesson 8), from information students may not have observed, and from the observations of other students. If students have not mentioned watering plants, lead the discussion to the amount of water that each soil sample might hold.

5. Direct students' attention to the fourth step of the wheel: Design and Conduct the Experiment. Tell students they are going to conduct an experiment to determine how much water different types of soil can absorb.

6. As a hypothesis, ask each group to rank its soil samples in order from least absorbent to most absorbent. Tell students to complete the sentence, "We predict that the order of soil samples from least absorbent to most absorbent will be . . . "

7. Lead groups through the experiment process with the sample of rocks/gravel. Tell students to write down the steps of the experiment in their log books so they can repeat the steps exactly with each of their other soil samples.
   - Place the filter paper over the top of the jar. Make a shallow dent in the middle to hold the soil. Put a rubber band around the top of the jar to hold the filter paper in place.
   - Fill the dent with some of the soil sample, in this case, rocks/gravel.
   - Carefully measure ¼ cup of water.
   - Slowly pour the water evenly over the soil sample. One group member should be watching the jar under the sample while the water is being poured.
   - Record observations:
     - What happens when the water is poured?
     - What does the sample look, feel, and smell like after the water has been poured?

   - Carefully remove the filter paper with the soil sample.
   - Pour the water in the bottom of the jar into the beaker (or measuring cup).
   - How much of the original ¼ cup of water is left?

8. Instruct students to follow the same steps with each of the soil samples. Encourage them to be methodical and detailed when recording their observations.

9. Once students have completed the experiment with all soil types, allow them to share their observations with the class. Make sure the following observations are mentioned:
   - Pouring the water on the rocks/gravel did not change their look, feel, or smell. Most of the water ran through them to the bottom of the jar.
   - The clay soaked up most of the water. (If the clay is tight, it will not get wet or damp on the bottom.) The clay became very plastic/sticky when wet.
   - The sand let most of the water run through it. When wet, it stuck together but crumbled easily. The sand still felt rough even when wet.
   - The topsoil absorbed some of the water but also let some water run through. When wet, it stuck together but pulled apart easily. The topsoil felt sponge-like when wet.

10. Direct students' attention to the fifth step on the wheel: Create Meaning. Instruct students to think about their observations and the class' discussion, asking:
    - Why do you think the ability of soil to absorb water might be important?

11. Lead students to discuss the importance of soil water for plants, asking:
    - What do plants need to grow? (Make sure they understand that plants need water and nutrients—food—to grow.)
    - Is this statement true or false: "Plants can never have too much water"? Why is it false?
    - Based on your experiment, which type of soil do you think would be best for plants? Why?

12. Tell students there is another reason why the topsoil (potting soil) is the best choice for plants. Remind students that plants need water *and* nutrients. Ask them if they know where plants get nutrients.

13. Use a small spade to scoop out some soil from the potted plant. Put the soil in the jar. Fill the jar nearly full with water and put on the lid. Shake the jar vigorously. Once the soil settles, direct students' attention to the top of the water. Ask students:
    - What do you see on top of the water?
    - What do you think it is? Why does it float?

14. Ask for a volunteer to use a net or filter paper to scoop out some of the floating material for each group. Allow each group a few minutes to investigate the substance. Ask students:
    - Now what do you think is in the floating layer? What do you recognize?

15. Explain to students that topsoil contains many rotting plant and animal materials. These rotting materials are called *humus*. It is the humus that nourishes the plant. Humus also helps hold the topsoil together so that it retains just the right amount—not too much and not too little—water. Post the word humus on the word wall.

16. Lead students in creating a concept map on soil classifications.

17. To begin this activity, tell students: "Let's review what we now understand about soil and illustrate our understanding with a new concept map." Show them the slide of Handout 9A (Soil Types Blank Concept Map) or distribute copies of Handout 9A. (Handout 9B shows an example of a completed concept map.) Tell students: "We know that soil comes in different varieties." Use the

following questions as a guide for completing the concept map activity. Model on the slide with Handout 9A as students work with their own copy.
- What do we know about soil? (Answer: It consists of different types.)
- What do the different types of soil include?
- What is different about these different types?

Concluding and Extending the Lesson

Concluding Questions and/or Actions
- Students can answer the following questions in discussion format or as journal entries in their log books:
  - Do all plants need the same amount of water? How do you know?
  - What kind of soil do you think we will need for a garden we could plan for Queen Anne's Island? Why?
  - What generalizations about change apply to soil?

What to Do at Home
- Direct students' attention to the sixth step on the wheel: Tell Others What Was Found. Instruct them to go home and share the results of their experiments with their parents.
- After getting permission, students should take some soil samples from their yard, then set up the experiment they did in class to check the porosity of different soil samples from their backyard. Students should use this information to advise their parents on where they should place plants.
- Suggest to students that different plants need different amounts of water. Encourage them to do some research using the Internet, books, magazines, and other resources to determine what kinds of plants need a lot of water versus those that need only a little water.
- Have students look at different vegetation and land in their neighborhoods and describe their characteristics.

Name:_____ Date:_____

Soil Types Blank Concept Map

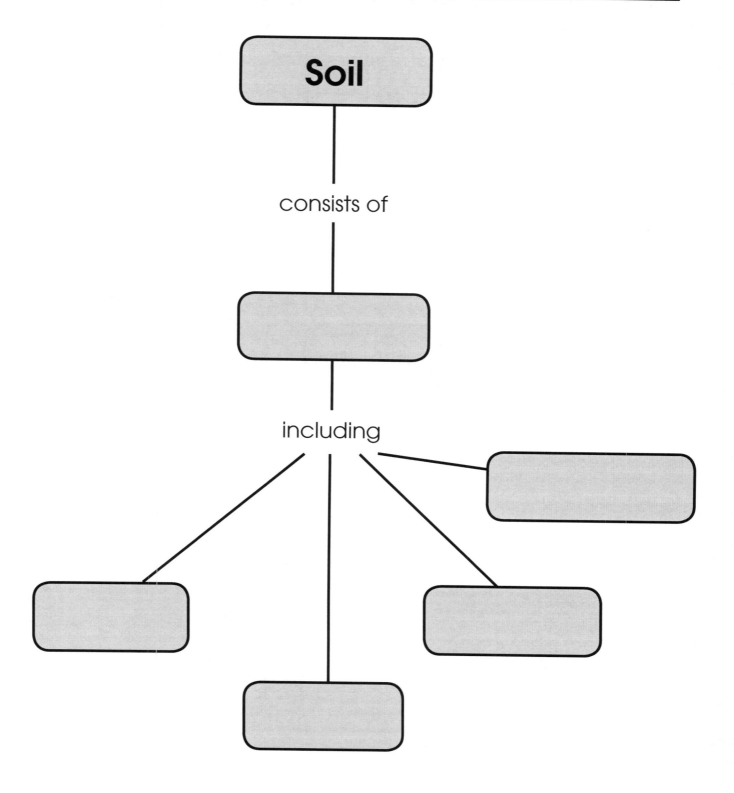

Soil

consists of

including

Name:_____ Date:_____

Soil Types Completed
Concept Map

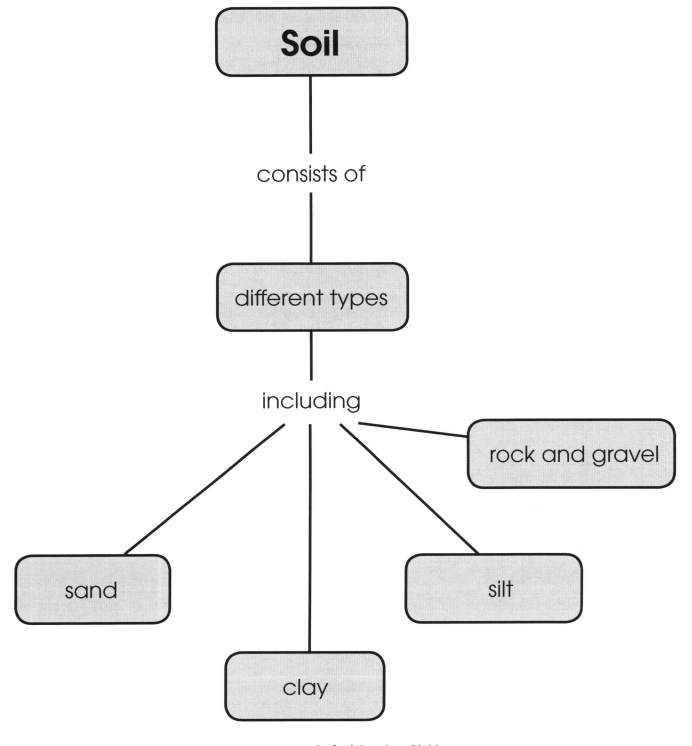

Lesson 10:
Soil Erosion

Planning the Lesson

Instructional Purpose
- To conduct an experiment with soil erosion.
- To connect the erosion process with the weathering process that breaks down rock to create soil over time.
- To discuss the possible drawbacks to erosion and how to prevent it.

Instructional Time
- 45 minutes

Change Concept Generalizations
- Change is everywhere.
- Change is related to time.
- Change can be natural or manmade.
- Change may be random or predictable.

Key Science Concepts
- Human activity affects the quality of air, water, and habitats.
- Topsoil is the upper soil surface and a natural product of the subsoil and bedrock.
- Subsoil and bedrock are layers of soil under the topsoil from which topsoil is formed over a long period of time by the action of water.
- Over time, weather, water, and living things break down rocks and create soil.

Scientific Investigation Skills and Processes
- Make observations.
- Ask questions.
- Learn more.
- Design and conduct experiments.
- Create meaning.
- Tell others what was found.

Assessment "Look Fors"
- Students can apply the steps of the scientific investigation process.
- Students show understanding of the process of erosion.
- Students can distinguish between natural erosion and erosion that is manmade.

Materials/Resources/Equipment
- Handout 10A (Message From Geologist #2), recorded on tape
- Slide of Handout 3A (Wheel of Scientific Investigation and Reasoning)
- Two large aluminum pans full of soil
- One large aluminum pan, empty
- Scissors
- Several large books

- Twigs with leaves to use as trees and plants
- Other objects to use as barriers to erosion (choose versatile items that could represent a number of student suggestions)
- Hair dryer
- Watering can full of water
- Extra water (if you don't have a sink in your classroom)
- Student log books
- United Streaming video clip: *Geologist's Notebook: Making a Mud Pie* (11 minutes).
- Word for word wall: erosion

Implementing the Lesson

1. Tell students you have received another message from the geologist. Play the recorded message.
2. Tell students that you are going to conduct an experiment to help out the geologist and other scientists on the island. Direct students' attention to the Wheel of Scientific Investigation and Reasoning (Handout 3A). Lead them through the first three steps, then ask:
   - What can we observe about the geologist's message?
   - What questions do we need to ask in order to help him or her?
   - How can we learn more?

3. Tell students that you will conduct a demonstration to show erosion and how it affects soil.
4. Ask students, "What is erosion?" Share the definition of the word *erosion*, and post the word erosion on the word wall.
5. Show students a pan of soil. Tell students that the pan of soil used to be covered by a forest, but humans have cut down all of the trees to use as building lumber, to make paper, and so on (make connections to the book *Common Ground* from Lesson 4). Ask a volunteer to describe the soil to the rest of the class. Place the soil on a table in the front of the room where everyone can see. Use the hair dryer to simulate wind blowing over the soil. Tell students to record their observations in their log books. Ask students:
   - What happens to the soil when the wind blows?

6. Explain to the students that they have seen an example of wind erosion. Ask students:
   - What would eventually happen if the wind continued to blow?
   - How might we stop or slow down wind erosion?

7. Choose one or two of the students' suggestions to test out. For example, students may suggest that the soil will not blow away as easily if it is wet. Use water to wet the soil and test their prediction. Also, students may suggest that if there were trees and other plants in the soil it wouldn't blow away as easily. Use small clippings from trees/shrubs to represent plant life and test their prediction. Ask students:
   - How might human actions have contributed to the wind erosion problem?

8. Keep a list of suggestions for combating wind erosion on the board or on chart paper.

9. Tell students you will now demonstrate a different type of erosion (water erosion). Show students the second pan of soil. Tell students that, like the previous soil, this pan used to be a forest but humans have cut down all of the trees for their own use (again, make connections to the book *Common Ground* from Lesson 4). Use several books to elevate one end of the pan of soil. Poke five or six holes in the other end of the soil using scissors. Then, place the nonelevated end of the pan into the empty pan (to catch water runoff).

10. Ask a student volunteer to describe the soil. Use the watering can to "rain" on the soil. Ask students to record their observations in their log books as it continues to rain. Discuss the following:
    - What happened when it rained on the bare soil? Why?
    - Why might water erosion be a bad thing?
    - What might we be able to do to prevent water erosion?

11. Choose one or two of the students' suggestions to test. For example, students may suggest that planting trees and other plants will help hold the soil in place and prevent water erosion. Use clippings from trees and shrubs to represent plants. See if less water erosion occurs. Ask students:
    - How have human actions contributed to the problems caused by water erosion?

> **Note to Teacher:**
> Before testing students' suggestions for preventing water erosion, replace the already wet soil with dry soil.

12. Add students' suggestions for combating water erosion to the list on the board/chart paper.

13. Direct students' attention to the fifth step on the wheel: Create Meaning. Ask students:
    - What meaning can we create from today's experiment?
    - What have you learned today that might help us solve the geologist's problem?
    - How will this information be helpful when we begin planning Preservation Park?

14. Tell students that the processes they just witnessed are the same processes by which mountains and other huge rocks are worn down to create soil. Over a very long period of time, wind, water, and other natural occurrences such as hurricanes, tornadoes, volcanoes, and earthquakes cause massive rocks to erode. The pieces that are eroded off these large rocks become the subsoil. They then mix with organic materials—such as dead plants and animals—to form the topsoil. Ask students:
    - Should we try to stop all erosion? Why or why not?

Concluding and Extending the Lesson

Concluding Questions and/or Actions
- How does erosion relate to our change generalizations?
- Have students write a letter or an e-mail to the geologist with suggestions for solving the erosion problem on Queen Anne's Island. Tell students to make sure they reassure the geologist that erosion will be one of the major considerations when developing Preservation Park.
- Show the United Streaming video clip *Geologist's Notebook: Making a Mud Pie*, which explains the formation of soil through different types of weathering.

What to Do at Home

- Tell students to walk around their backyard, neighborhood, nearby forest, and other nearby pieces of land. They should look for examples of naturally occurring erosion and erosion caused by human actions. If possible, students should take pictures using a digital camera. Have students answer the following questions: Why do you think each type of erosion occurred? Should any steps be taken to prevent any of the erosion in your examples? Why or why not?

Name:_____ Date:_____

Message From Geologist #2

Hi there, scientists! Are you working hard in preparation for designing Preservation Park on Queen Anne's Island? Hope so! Did you know that soil is one of our most precious natural resources? Well, it is, and we have a problem here on the island. Every day more and more of our soil gets eroded away! How can we stop this from happening? We need your help!

Lesson 11:
Land Pollution: Garbage!

Planning the Lesson

Instructional Purpose
- To discuss the issue of land pollution (waste disposal).
- To investigate the types of waste that students dispose of at school.
- To articulate solutions to land pollution problems.

Instructional Time
- 45 minutes

Change Concept Generalizations
- Change is everywhere.
- Change is related to time.
- Change can be natural or manmade.

Key Science Concepts
- Human activity affects the quality of air, water, and habitats.
- Conservation and resource renewal protect the quality and quantity of natural resources.

Scientific Investigation Skills and Processes
- Make observations.
- Ask questions.
- Learn more.

Assessment "Look Fors"
- Students can apply the steps of the scientific investigation process.
- Students show understanding of the issue of land pollution.
- Students can articulate possible solutions to the problem of land pollution.

Materials/Resources/Equipment
- *Where Does the Garbage Go?* by Paul Showers
- Slide and one copy per student of Handout 11A (Garbage Data Collection Table)
- Plastic drop cloth
- Signs labeled "Food and Yard Waste," "Glass," "Metal," "Paper," "Plastic," and "Other"
- Plastic gloves, one pair for each student
- Large bag of nonhazardous garbage (collect trash from neighboring classrooms for a few days)
- Six garbage bags
- Bathroom scale
- Markers
- "Sarah Cynthia Sylvia Stout Would Not Take the Garbage Out" by Shel Silverstein
- Student log books

> **Note to Teacher:**
> Students can be directed to copy the Garbage Data Collection Table in their log books if you do not want to photocopy the chart for each student.

Implementing the Lesson

1. Ask students, "What is pollution? What is land pollution?"
2. Read *Where Does the Garbage Go?* by Paul Showers. Allow students to answer the questions in the book as you are reading.
3. Tell students that they are going to investigate the school's trash today. Ask students:
   - How can we gather information about the school's garbage?
   - What kind of waste do you throw away each day?

4. Create a large garbage collection center at the front of the class by spreading out the plastic drop cloth. Ask a few student volunteers to divide the drop cloth into sections using the signs labeled with different types of waste.
5. Give each student a pair of plastic gloves.
6. Weigh the unseparated bag of garbage. Write the total weight on the board. Divide students in small groups of four or five. Allow each group to take some garbage from the big bag and sort it into the categories provided by the labels on the plastic drop cloth.
7. After students have sorted all of the garbage, ask for volunteers to bag up each category. Make sure they carefully label each bag so as not to mix up the different types of garbage.
8. Ask for more volunteers to weigh each bag of separated garbage. Record the weight of each type of garbage on the Garbage Data Collection Table (Handout 11A). Ask students to record the weights on their copies of the table. Then, if students have learned percentages, instruct them to divide the weight of each bag by the total weight of the garbage and then multiply by 100. The resulting number is the percentage of all garbage that is comprised of one particular category (e.g., they may find that paper waste is 50% of the school's total waste).
9. Discuss with students the findings from their study on the school's waste. Ask students:
   - Were you surprised by any of the findings? Why or why not?
   - Why is it important to analyze waste disposal?
   - What are the implications of waste disposal on air and water quality, habitats, and living creatures?
   - How does our school's waste contribute to these implications?
   - What are some things we can do to change or limit our waste disposal practices?

10. Read aloud the poem, "Sarah Cynthia Sylvia Stout Would Not Take the Garbage Out" by Shel Silverstein.
11. Instruct students to write a letter to Sarah Cynthia Sylvia Stout explaining to her that she is polluting our land. Tell students to make sure they explain the land pollution problem to her and to give her suggestions for ways she can help minimize the amount of waste she produces.

Concluding and Extending the Lesson

Concluding Questions and/or Actions

- How might land pollution have contributed to the problem on Queen Anne's Island?
- How might land pollution be a problem for Preservation Park? How can we prevent these problems before they occur?

- What, if any, change generalizations apply to land pollution? Explain your answer.
- Use a software program like Excel to create a data table of percentages. Then, using the graphing feature, turn the data table into a pie chart.

What to Do at Home
- Ask students to talk with their parents and siblings about:
    - the kind of waste that their family produces,
    - the problem of land pollution and how their family can be part of the solution, and
    - ways that their family can reduce the amount of waste produced.

- Encourage students to start a waste reduction program in their homes (with their parents' permission).

Name:_____ Date:_____

Garbage Data Collection Table

Type of Garbage	Weight	Percentage of Total
Food and Yard Waste		
Glass		
Metal		
Paper		
Plastic		
Other		
Total		100%

Lesson 12:
Oil Spill!

Planning the Lesson

Instructional Purpose
- To illustrate the effects of a manmade disaster—an oil spill—on Earth's natural resources.
- To make inferences about how an oil spill might affect Queen Anne's Island and about the best method for cleaning up oil spills.

Instructional Time
- 45 minutes

Change Concept Generalizations
- Change can be natural or manmade.
- Change may be random or predictable.

Key Science Concepts
- Sources of energy on Earth include sunlight, water, and wind.
- Some natural energy resources are renewable and some are not.
- Human activity affects the quality of air, water, and habitats.
- Conservation and resource renewal protect the quality and quantity of natural resources.

Scientific Investigation Skills and Processes
- Make observations.
- Ask questions.
- Learn more.
- Design and conduct experiments.
- Create meaning.
- Tell others what was found.

Assessment "Look Fors"
- Students can apply the steps of the scientific investigation process.
- Students can identify the causes and effects of water pollution on wildlife and the environment.

Materials/Resources/Equipment
- *Oil Spill!* by Melvin Berger
- Slide of Handout 3A (the Scientific Wheel of Investigation and Reasoning)
- Copies of Handout 12A (Oil Spill Cleanup Experiment Log), one per student
- Copies of Handout 12B (Experimental Report Form), one per student
- Small disposable pans, four per group with each separately labeled "water," "A," "B," and "C"
- Containers of water at room temperature, one per group
- Containers of vegetable oil, one per group
- Drop cloth (or sufficient newspaper) to place under pans, one per group
- Roll of paper towels, one per group
- Containers of liquid dish soap, one per group

- Containers of baking soda, one per group
- Feathers (craft or real), 12–15 per group
- Plastic spoons, two per group (to measure dish soap and baking soda)
- Student log books
- Scientific Investigation Badges, one per student printed on colored paper or labels and laminated (optional)

Implementing the Lesson

1. Tell students that this lesson will focus on one of our more abundant and also more precious natural resources—water—and the changes that can happen when humans make a mistake.

2. Read aloud *Oil Spill!* by Melvin Berger. As you read, ask students:
   - What was spilled? (Lead students to realize that oil is a natural resource that has gone through or will go through a refinement process.)
   - How do oil spills happen?
   - How do oil spills affect the plants and animals in the ocean?
   - How do these effects on ocean life in turn affect other parts of our environment?
   - What are some ways scientists clean up oil spills? Do you think there is one method that works better than others? Why or why not?
   - How might we prevent oil spills?

3. Tell students they are going to conduct an experiment about an oil spill. Direct students' attention to the first step on the wheel: Make Observations. Ask them to think about the book and the class discussion. Ask students to record their observations about oil spills in their log books.

4. Direct students' attention to the second step on the wheel: Ask Questions. Ask students to respond to the following question in their log books:
   - What kinds of questions can you ask about oil spills? About cleaning up oil spills?

5. Direct students' attention to the third step on the wheel: Learn More. Ask students what they have already learned about cleaning up oil spills and then discuss the following:
   - How might we be able to find out more information to answer our questions about oil spills and cleaning them up?

6. Direct students' attention to the fourth step on the wheel: Design and Conduct the Experiment. Tell students they are going to conduct an experiment to answer the question, "What is the best method for removing oil from birds' feathers?"

7. Tell students they are going to test three methods: paper towels, dishwashing liquid, and baking soda.

8. Ask students to write their hypothesis in their log books. Have them complete the statement, "I think _____ will be the best way to clean oil from birds' feathers."

9. Divide students into groups of four. Each student in the group should be responsible for one step in the oil spill and clean-up experiment:
   - One student is assigned to cause the oil spill in the pan with the water and feathers.

- One student is assigned to clean the feathers with the paper towels, starting with one paper towel per feather. Students may wish to use additional paper towels. If so, they should record the number used.
- One student is assigned to clean the feathers with the baking soda, starting with one level spoonful. Students may wish to use additional spoonfuls. If so, they should record the number used.
- One student is assigned to clean the feathers with the dishwashing detergent, starting with one level spoonful. Students may wish to use additional spoonfuls. If so, they should record the number used.

10. Give each student a copy of the Oil Spill Cleanup Experiment Log (Handout 12A). Remind students that scientists collect their data carefully because they hope to use the data to create meaning.
11. Tell students that each group is going to conduct the experiment simultaneously. Then, guide the students through each step of the experiment beginning with the oil spill and then each cleanup method. Involve students in asking questions and making observations as they conduct each experiment. Guide students to use the materials appropriately.
12. Supply each group with newspaper/drop cloth, four disposable pans, one container each of water, vegetable oil, dish soap, and baking soda; one roll of paper towels; 12–15 feathers; and two spoons.
13. Spread out the newspaper or drop cloth for each group. Place all four pans on it. Arrange the pans in the following order:
    - Pan half full of room-temperature water
    - Pan labeled A (paper towels)
    - Pan labeled B (baking soda)
    - Pan labeled C (dish soap)
    - Pitcher of plain, room-temperature water

14. Ask the students responsible for the pan of room-temperature water to cause an oil spill by pouring the vegetable oil into the pan labeled "water." Then, ask them to submerge the feathers in the oil. Explain to students that the feathers represent sea birds that have been affected by an oil spill. Once the feathers have been submerged in the oil, the student should distribute the feathers into the pans labeled "A," "B," and "C."
15. Ask the students responsible for the pan labeled A to test the first cleaning method by attempting to clean the feathers in pan A using paper towels. Tell the other students to record their observations on their Oil Spill Cleanup Experiment Log. Allow students to share their observations while the volunteer continues to try to clean the feathers. Place the paper-towel-cleaned feathers in front of pan A.
16. Ask the students responsible for the pan labeled B to test the second cleaning method by attempting to clean the feathers in pan B using the baking soda. Tell them they may mix the baking soda with water from the pitcher if they wish. The other students should record their observations on their Oil Spill Cleanup Experiment Log. Allow students to share their observations while the volunteer continues to try to clean the feathers. Place the feathers cleaned with baking soda in front of pan B.
17. Ask the students responsible for the pan labeled C to test the third cleaning method—liquid dish soap—in the pan labeled C. Students may use water from the pitcher with this method as well. Ask the rest of the students to record and share their observations. Place the feather cleaned with dish soap in front of pan C.

18. Once all of the methods have been tested, direct students' attention to the fifth step on the wheel: Create Meaning. Ask students to complete the sections on their Experiment Log titled "What did you learn from this experiment?" and "What additional questions do you have?" Give students the Experimental Report Form (Handout 12B) and ask them to fill it out.

19. Ask students:
   - Based on the experiment, what is the best method for cleaning oil from birds' feathers? Why?
   - Did you come to the same conclusion as the other groups? If not, why?

20. As a whole class, discuss how what students have learned might be helpful to other people:
   - Do you think other people would benefit from knowing what you have learned? How so?
   - Do you think knowing about this experiment would make people want to prevent future oil spills? Why or why not?
   - How can we communicate our findings to other people? How can we help everyone work toward preventing future oil spills?

21. Give each student a Scientific Investigation Badge (optional).

Concluding and Extending the Lesson

Concluding Questions and/or Actions
   - What was the purpose of our investigation, and how does it relate to real-world conservation issues?
   - What criteria did you use to determine which method was best for removing the oil from the birds' feathers?
   - What can you infer from the experiment about the best method for removing oil from birds' feathers in a real oil spill?
   - Which change generalizations apply to our oil spill and our experiment findings?
   - How do you think an oil spill might affect the natural resources on Queen Anne's Island?
   - What additional research would you like to conduct on oil spills?

What to Do at Home
   - Ask students to conduct research on the Exxon Valdez oil spill and the different methods used for cleaning up the oil in this spill.
   - Encourage students to design a new experiment to test alternatives to methods used in this investigation with their parents' permission.
   - Ask students to identify some sources of water pollution in their daily lives. Students should answer these questions in their log books:
     - Which of these sources is most preventable?
     - How can you help decrease water pollution?

   - Indicate to students that they should be prepared to share what they learned with the class.

Name:_____ Date:_____

Oil Spill Cleanup Experiment Log

Hypothesis:		
	Amount Used	**Observations**
Pan A **Paper Towels**		
Pan B **Baking Soda**		
Pan C **Dish Soap**		
What did you learn from this experiment?		
What additional questions do you have?		

Name:_____ Date:_____

Experimental Report Form

Name of Experiment _____

1. What was your hypothesis (or prediction about what would happen)?

2. What materials did you use to test the hypothesis?

3. What methods did you use? (Outline your steps.)

4. What data have been collected? Where are your data recorded? (Attach your data table.)

5. What are your findings? (Did your hypothesis prove to be true or false?)

6. What new questions do you have?

Science Investigation Badges

I Conducted an
Experiment in
Science—
Ask Me
About It!

I Conducted an
Experiment in
Science—
Ask Me
About It!

I Conducted an
Experiment in
Science—
Ask Me
About It!

I Conducted an
Experiment in
Science—
Ask Me
About It!

I Conducted an
Experiment in
Science—
Ask Me
About It!

I Conducted an
Experiment in
Science—
Ask Me
About It!

Lesson 13:
Planning Preservation Park

Planning the Lesson

Instructional Purpose
- To guide students to begin to connect everything they have learned in this unit to develop a plan for Preservation Park on Queen Anne's Island.

Note to Teacher:
If you wish, students may be given two 45-minute class periods to prepare for their presentation in Lesson 14.

Instructional Time
- 45 minutes—If students need more time to create their final products, you may wish to allot more time for this lesson.

Change Concept Generalizations
- Change is everywhere.
- Change is related to time.
- Change can be natural or manmade.
- Change may be random or predictable.

Key Science Concepts
- Sources of energy on Earth include sunlight, water, and wind.
- Some natural energy resources are renewable and some are not.
- Human activity affects the quality of air, water, and habitats.
- Conservation and resource renewal protect the quality and quantity of natural resources.
- Humans depend on several major sources of energy found on Earth.
- Soil provides support and nutrients for plants.
- Rock, clay, silt, sand, and humus are components of soil.
- Topsoil is the upper soil surface and a natural product of the subsoil and bedrock.

Scientific Investigation Skills and Processes
- Make observations.
- Create meaning.
- Tell others what was found.

Assessment "Look Fors"
- Students can make connections between lessons on soil, natural resources, and energy sources.
- Students understand that creativity applies new knowledge to the development of a plan to protect natural resources.
- Students can work collaboratively with others.

Materials/Resources/Equipment
- *Someday a Tree* by Eve Bunting
- Handout 13A (Message From Geologist #3), previously recorded
- Scratch paper and/or graph paper
- Poster board or trifold boards, one per group

Note to Teacher:
Instead of a poster board or trifold board, software such as PowerPoint also could be used for the final presentation.

- Markers, colored pencils, glue, paint, and other art supplies
- Student log books

Implementing the Lesson

1. Read aloud the book *Someday a Tree* by Eve Bunting. Discuss with students how this story relates to everything they have learned about soil, natural resources, and energy sources.
2. During your discussion about the book, have another teacher, a teacher's assistant, or one of the office staff come into your room with a tape with the final message from the geologist. Play the recording for students.
3. Tell students the moment of truth has arrived! Divide them into groups of three to five. Tell each student to keep his or her log book at hand as the students will need to access the information they have learned about soil, natural resources, and energy sources.
4. Give each group some scratch paper and/or graph paper. Give them time to design their versions of Preservation Park.
5. Approve each group's plan before allowing it to move to the next step. Ensure that students have addressed the three major components mentioned by the geologist: soil, natural resources, and energy sources.
6. Give each group a poster board or a trifold board. Instruct students to transfer their plans for Preservation Park to the presentation board. Remind students that they are trying to "sell" their ideas to the Preservation Park Planning Committee. Their presentations need to be carefully planned and executed. In addition to presenting their designs, make sure students explain why they made the choices they made.

Concluding and Extending the Lesson

Concluding Questions and/or Actions

- Have you addressed the composition of the soil in Preservation Park? The issue of soil erosion?
- Have you addressed the issue of protecting and renewing natural resources within the park?
- Have you addressed the issue of energy to provide power for tasks such as watering plants, running water fountains, powering lights for evenings in the park, and so on?
- What is unique about your park design? Why do you think the planning committee should choose your plan?
- Have students create their own map of Queen Anne's Island and Preservation Park.
- What generalizations about change apply to the preservation of the park?

What to Do at Home

- Ask students to discuss the following questions with their families:
  1. Which clothing will be a good choice to wear when making the presentation to the Preservation Park Planning Committee?
  2. Why is it important to choose clothing carefully?
  3. Why did you suggest this clothing?

- Encourage students to delve deeper into the preservation park planning by generating ideas to share with their groups about ways they can improve their group's approaches to soil planning, natural resource preservation, and energy supply in the park.

Name: _____ Date: _____

Message From Geologist #3

Well, scientists, the time has come. I'm afraid we can't wait any longer to begin planning Preservation Park. Queen Anne's Island desperately needs a plan to protect and renew its natural resources. The Preservation Park Planning Committee will be meeting soon. You need to be ready to present your ideas to them. They are most interested in hearing about your plans for the soil, the preservation of natural resources, and the most environmentally friendly use of energy. I can't wait to hear your ideas!

Lesson 14:
Preservation Park
Planning Committee

Planning the Lesson

Instructional Purpose
- To help students demonstrate their understanding of the concepts covered in this unit: soil, natural resources, the renewal of natural resources, and energy sources, particularly solar energy.

Instructional Time
- 45 minutes

Change Concept Generalizations
- Change is everywhere.
- Change is related to time.
- Change can be natural or manmade.
- Change may be random or predictable.

Key Science Concepts
- Sources of energy on Earth include sunlight, water, and wind.
- Some natural energy resources are renewable and some are not.
- Human activity affects the quality of air, water, and habitats.
- Conservation and resource renewal protect the quality and quantity of natural resources.
- Fossil fuels are formed from decayed plants and animals.
- Humans depend on several major sources of energy found on Earth.
- Soil provides support and nutrients for plants.
- Rock, clay, silt, sand, and humus are components of soil.
- Topsoil is the upper soil surface and a natural product of the subsoil and bedrock.
- Subsoil refers to the layers of soil under the topsoil from which topsoil is formed over a long period of time by the action of the water.
- Over time, weather, water, and living things help break down rocks and create soil.

Scientific Investigation Skills and Processes
- Tell others what was found.

Assessment "Look Fors"
- Students demonstrate an understanding of the key science concepts.
- Students demonstrate an understanding of the relationship between the planning of Preservation Park and the concept of change.
- Students can articulate ideas clearly and coherently.

Materials/Resources/Equipment
- Group posters or trifolds

- Copies of Handout 14A (Presentation Rubric)
- Handout 14B (Preservation Expert Badges), copied on color paper or labels and laminated (optional)

Implementing the Lesson

1. Tell students that the time has come to pitch their designs for Preservation Park to the Preservation Park Planning Committee. To add to the authenticity of the scenario, consider assembling a group of adults to serve as the committee during the students' presentations.
2. Remind students that they need to address three major concepts in their presentations: natural resources, soil, and energy sources. Remind them also that they must provide an explanation to the committee for the choices they made in the Preservation Park design.
3. Allow each group 5–10 minutes to present their designs and their design rationales.
4. Use the Presentation Rubric (Handout 14A) to score each group's presentation.
5. If desired, allow the Planning Committee to choose the plan that best addresses each concept and the best plan overall.
6. Tell students they are officially Preservation Experts and distribute Preservation Expert Badges (Handout 14B). Congratulate them on a job well done!

Concluding and Extending the Lesson

Concluding Questions and/or Actions

- Now that this unit is over, how can you apply what you have learned to other aspects of your life? How can you continue to address the issue of natural resource preservation in the future?
- How do the change generalizations apply to what you have learned about soil, natural resources, and energy sources?
- In what ways might you change your plan for Preservation Park to make it stronger?
- In what ways have you become a better scientist?
- Ask students to help you make a list of science words (concepts) that were used in this lesson. Tell students to talk with a partner about these words and what each of them means. Then ask for volunteers to use one of the words in a sentence that talks about something they learned in the lesson. Create a chart of sentences.

What to Do at Home

- Ask students to think about their group's design for Preservation Park and the designs of the other teams. Ask them to identify the elements of the designs that they could implement at home. Encourage them to discuss their ideas with their families, and then to implement one or two ideas in their homes in order to do their part toward preserving and renewing the Earth's resources.

Name: _____ Date: _____

Handout 14A
Presentation Rubric

	Below Expectations	Meets Expectations	Exceeds Expectations
Addresses the type of soil that should be used in the park. Includes information about soil components, including rock, clay, silt, sand, and humus. Also discusses the importance of rich topsoil.			
Addresses the importance of protecting natural resources such as water, soil, plants, fossil fuels, and rocks on Queen Anne's Island. Develops ideas to protect these resources within the park and ways to ensure the renewal of renewable resources.			
Addresses the source of energy necessary to run the park (e.g., lights, sprinkler systems, water fountains, decorative fountains, etc.). Uses alternate energy sources when appropriate.			
Provides reasonable rationale for all choices made.			
Clearly and coherently articulates park design and rationale.			

Preservation Expert Badges

I'm a
Preservation
Expert—
Ask Me
About It!

I'm a
Preservation
Expert—
Ask Me
About It!

I'm a
Preservation
Expert—
Ask Me
About It!

I'm a
Preservation
Expert—
Ask Me
About It!

I'm a
Preservation
Expert—
Ask Me
About It!

I'm a
Preservation
Expert—
Ask Me
About It!

Lesson 15:
Wrap It Up!

Planning the Lesson

Instructional Purpose
- To summarize conceptual understanding, key science concepts, and the scientific investigation process.

Instructional Time
- 60 minutes

Change Concept Generalizations
- Change is everywhere.
- Change is related to time.
- Change can be natural or manmade.
- Change may be random or predictable.

Key Science Concepts
- Sources of energy on Earth include sunlight, water, and wind.
- Some natural energy resources are renewable and some are not.
- Human activity affects the quality of air, water, and habitats.
- Conservation and resource renewal protect the quality and quantity of natural resources.
- Humans depend on several major sources of energy found on Earth.
- Fossil fuels are formed from decayed plants and animals.
- Soil provides support and nutrients for plants.
- Rock, clay, silt, sand, and humus are components of soil.
- Topsoil is the upper soil surface and a natural product of the subsoil and bedrock.
- Subsoil and bedrock are layers of soil under the topsoil from which topsoil is formed over a long period of time by the action of water.
- Over time, weather, water, and living things help break down rocks and create soil.

Scientific Investigation Skills and Processes
- Make observations.
- Ask questions.
- Learn more.
- Design and conduct experiments.
- Create meaning.
- Tell others what was found.

Assessment "Look Fors"
- Students should be able to describe how change occurs in natural resources and how humans change the environment.
- Students should be able to draw a concept map for the key science concepts and terms used in the unit.

- Students should be able to describe the scientific investigation process and explain its application to the macroconcept and the key science concepts in the unit.

Materials/Resources/Equipment
- Student log books
- Chart paper
- Markers
- Small plant
- Cup, large enough to cover the plant and that will enclose the plant in darkness
- Copies of Handout 12B (Experimental Report Form), or slide for class viewing

Implementing the Lesson

1. Wrap up the student log books:
   - Review the log books with the students. Show them a segment from a famous scientist's log book (such as Salk) to give them the idea that all scientists use logs in their work.
   - Discuss any questions about log entries that they have.

2. Wrap up the problem:
   - Revisit the original problem scenario and yesterday's activity and ask:
     - How did we solve the problem?
     - How did we work as a team?
     - If we had more time or resources, what might the next step be?
     - What might we have done differently?

   - Make sure students understand that finding a solution often takes scientists many years. Explain that the work on Preservation Park could be the foundation for other scientists to explore.
   - Discuss the process that is used to research a solution, test a solution, and get it to market. Explain that the time that lapses between discovery and end product is very long.

3. Wrap up the change concept:
   - Ask pairs of students to:
     - Give examples from the unit of how change happens over time.
     - Give examples of change in their environment.
     - Categorize the examples as natural or manmade.

   - Pick three pairs of students to share.

4. Wrap up the key science concepts:
   - Review the key science concepts and terms from the word bank with students.
   - Divide students into groups. Ask each group of students to create a concept map on one of the concepts, such as energy sources or natural resources. Students can use the chart paper and markers.
   - Ask three groups to present their concept maps.
   - Ask the remaining groups to discuss what they have learned by using concept maps.

5. Wrap up the scientific investigation process:
- Distribute Handout 12B, or show the slide of the page. Review the Experimental Report Form steps. Do a demonstration, using a paper cup to cover a plant. How long will it take for the plant to die? What do you predict? Work through the steps and discuss.
- Discuss the experiments you have done in the unit:
  - What questions have we asked?
  - What data sources have we used in the unit?
  - What types of hypotheses have we made?
  - What were some of our findings?
  - What did we learn from the investigations?
  - What did we learn about change from the investigations?

Concluding and Extending the Lesson

Concluding Questions
- In what ways has your thinking changed about natural resources and soil?
- We also discussed the concept of change. What have you learned about change from our investigations?

What to Do at Home
- Have students take home their log books and other unit materials. Tell them to share what they have learned with their parents.

Postassessment Directions
for the Teacher

Planning the Lesson

Instructional Purpose
- To assess student understanding of the unit macroconcept, student knowledge of the key science concepts in the unit, and student skills in the scientific investigation process.

Instructional Time
- Macroconcept assessment: 30 minutes
- Key science concepts assessment: 30 minutes
- Scientific process assessment: 20 minutes

Materials/Resources/Equipment
- Copies of postassessments for the unit (Postassessment for Change Concept, Postassessment for Key Science Concepts, and Postassessment for Scientific Process) for each student
- Exemplar Answers for the Postassessment for Change Concept, Exemplar Concept Maps of Soil for Postassessment for Key Science Concepts, and Exemplar Answers for the Postassessment for the Scientific Process
- Pencils
- Copies of blank concept map drawing sheet for each student

Implementing the Lesson
1. Give each student a copy of the postassessments to complete in the order noted above. The assessments should take no more than 80 minutes in all.
2. Explain that the assessment will be used to see how much students have learned during the unit.

Scoring
- Use the rubrics contained in the preassessment sections for concept, content, and scientific process. Sample exemplar responses are provided after each postassessment.

Name:_____ Date:_____

Postassessment for Change Concept

1. Give as many examples of things that change as you can (up to 10).

_____   _____

_____   _____

_____   _____

_____   _____

_____   _____

2. Draw one example of something that changes, showing before and after the change. Provide as many details as you can.

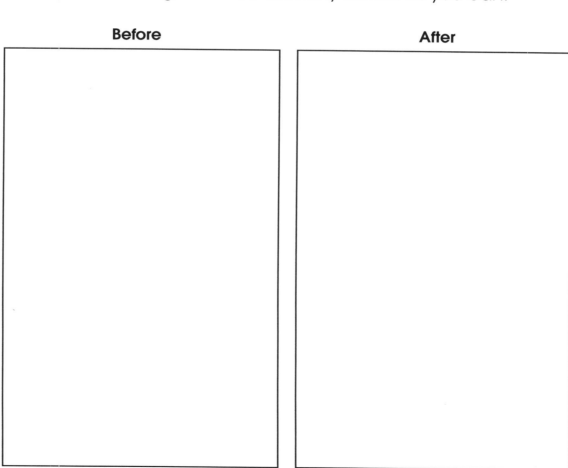

Before   **After**

3. Identify five ways that a tree could change or be changed.

_____

_____

_____

_____

_____

4. What are three things you can say about *all* change?

All change _____

_____

All change _____

_____

All change _____

_____

Exemplar Answers for Postassessment for the Change Concept

Note: Student answers may vary; these are simply to provide samples of quality postassessment answers to aid in scoring.

High Score

1. Give as many examples of things that change as you can (up to 10).
   Plants, People, Hair, Houses, Weather, Water, Soil, Animals, Paper, Crayons
2. Draw one example of something that changes, showing before and after.
   Before: Sunny weather; After: Rainy weather
3. Identify five ways that a tree could change or be changed.
   Cut down, Poisoned, Leaves turn color, Leaves fall off, Rats
4. What are three things you can say about *all* change?
   Happens at different times. Has a meaning for happening. Is good or bad.

Medium Score

1. Give as many examples of things that change as you can (up to 10).
   Frogs, Children, Plants, People, Animals, Trees, Birds, Larva, Moth, Hair, Butterfly
2. Draw one example of something that changes, showing before and after.
   Before: Egg; After: Bird
3. Identify five ways that a tree could change or be changed.
   Colors of leaves
4. What are three things you can say about *all* change?
   Butterflies change from a caterpillar. Frogs change from a tadpole. Flowers are seeds first, then it is a flower.

Low Score

1. Give as many examples of things that change as you can (up to 10).
   Tree, wood
2. Draw one example of something that changes, showing before and after.
   Before: Tree; After: Paper
3. Identify five ways that a tree could change or be changed.
   Firewood, cut
4. What are three things you can say about *all* change?
   (Left blank)

Postassessment for Key Science Concepts

Directions to the Teacher: Read the following paragraph to students:

Today I would like you to think about all of the things you know about soil. Think about the words you would use and the pictures you could draw to make a concept map. Think about the connections you can make. On your concept map paper, draw in pictures and words all that you know about soil. You will be drawing a concept map similar to those you have done before. Today's question is: "Tell me everything you know about soil."

Name: _____

Date: _____

Concept Map
Soil

Exemplar Concept Maps of Soil for Postassessment for Key Science Concepts

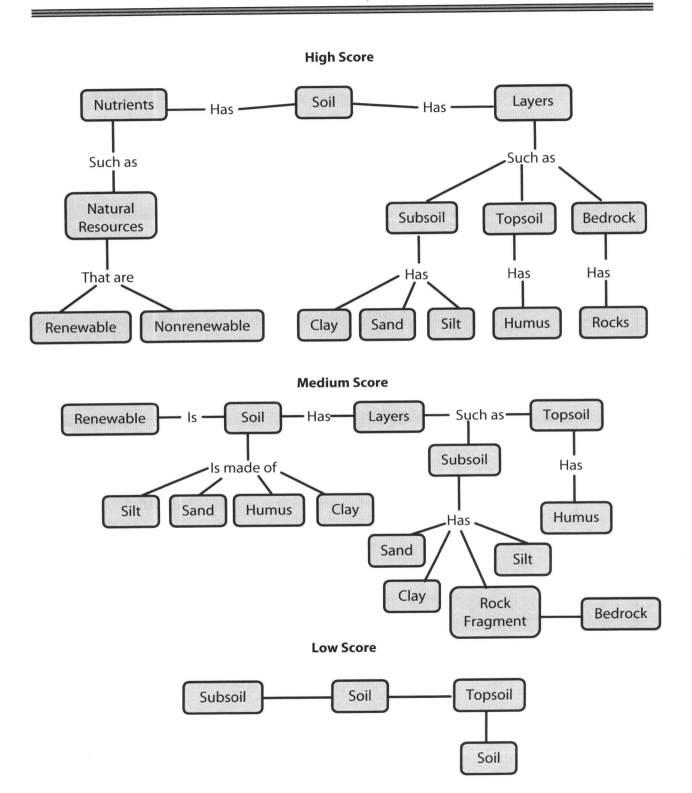

High Score

Nutrients — Has — Soil — Has — Layers

Nutrients — Such as — Natural Resources

Natural Resources — That are — Renewable / Nonrenewable

Layers — Such as — Subsoil / Topsoil / Bedrock

Subsoil — Has — Clay / Sand / Silt

Topsoil — Has — Humus

Bedrock — Has — Rocks

Medium Score

Renewable — Is — Soil — Has — Layers — Such as — Topsoil

Soil — Is made of — Silt / Sand / Humus / Clay

Layers — Subsoil

Subsoil — Has — Sand / Clay / Rock Fragment / Silt

Rock Fragment — Bedrock

Topsoil — Has — Humus

Low Score

Subsoil — Soil — Topsoil

Topsoil — Soil

Name:_____ Date:_____

Postassessment for Scientific Process

Directions: How would you study the question: How much water do plants need? Describe an experiment to test this question that includes the following:

   1. Prediction regarding the question (How much water do plants need?):

     I predict that_____

     _____

     _____

     _____.

   2. What materials will be needed to conduct the experiment?

     _____   _____

     _____   _____

     _____   _____

   3. What steps must be taken to conduct the experiment and *in what order?*

     a. _____

     b. _____

     c. _____

     d. _____

     e. _____

4. What data do you want to collect and how should they be recorded?

What will I collect?	How will I record the data?

5. How do the data help me decide if my prediction is correct? Explain.

_____

_____

_____

_____

Exemplar Answers for Postassessment for the Scientific Process

Note: Student answers may vary; these are simply to provide samples of quality postassessment answers to aid in scoring.

High Score

1. Prediction regarding the question (How much water do plants need?):
   I predict that you should give them 2 cups every week.
2. What materials will be needed to conduct the experiment?
   Plant, Sunlight, Soil, Fresh air, Water, Measuring cup
3. What steps must be taken to conduct the experiment and *in what order?*
   (a) Put a plant in soil. (b) Water it. (c) Put it in the sun. (d) Let it be in fresh air. (e) Water it every week.
4. What data do you want to collect and how should they be recorded?
   What will I collect? If I was right, I need more or less water in a certain amount of time.
   How will I record the data? In a log.
5. How do the data help me decide if my prediction is correct? Explain.
   If the plant is still alive.

Medium Score

1. Prediction regarding the question (How much water do plants need?):
   I predict that about 2 cups a day.
2. What materials will be needed to conduct the experiment?
   Soil, Water, Charts, Magnifying glass
3. What steps must be taken to conduct the experiment and *in what order?*
   (a) Get the soil. (b) Get the water. (c) Collect the data. (d) Write it down. (e) Share your data.
4. What data do you want to collect and how should they be recorded?
   What will I collect? How much water will be needed? What kind of soil?
   How will I record the data? Notebook.
5. How do the data help me decide if my prediction is correct? Explain.
   Research on the computer, science books.

Low Score

1. Prediction regarding the question (How much water do plants need?):
   I predict that not that much of a whole lot of water.
2. What materials will be needed to conduct the experiment?
   Water, Sunlight, Topsoil, Seeds, Garden, Nurturer
3. What steps must be taken to conduct the experiment and *in what order?*
   (a) First seeds to plant. (b) Then soil to help the plant. (c) Then sunlight. (d) Water. (e) Then cure.
4. What data do you want to collect and how should they be recorded?
   What will I collect? How much water plants need.
   How will I record the data? Science board.
5. How do the data help me decide if my prediction is correct? Explain.
   Give water. Water by day.

Appendix A
Concept Paper on Change

By Beverly T. Sher, Ph.D.

This paper was adapted from: Sher, B. T. (2004). Change. In J. L. VanTassel-Baska (Ed.), *Science key concepts* (pp. 31–35). Williamsburg, VA: Center for Gifted Education, The College of William and Mary.

We live in a changing world. Change and the absence of change are important features of both scientific and nonscientific processes. Change can occur in simple, predictable ways: Winter gradually gives way to spring, water evaporates from puddles after the rain ends, the sun rises and sets, we (well, most of us, anyway) change from a state of sleep at night to being awake in the daytime. It also can occur in more complicated and unpredictable ways: Hemlines rise and fall apparently randomly, the stock market gyrates, mutations resulting in changed organisms occur, the weather changes. It can also fail to occur: A bottle of root beer in the pantry, when opened, contains the same amount of liquid that it had months earlier at the bottling plant; healthy people maintain roughly the same body temperature at all times (with small, cyclic, daily variations); a rock formation photographed a year ago has the same contours now as it did then. In this concept paper, we will explore the concept of change and the related concept of equilibrium.

There are four general patterns of change. They include:
1. Steady changes: changes that occur at a characteristic rate.
2. Cyclic changes: changes that repeat in cycles.
3. Random changes: changes that occur irregularly, unpredictably, and in a way that is mathematically random.
4. Chaotic changes: changes that appear random and irregular on the surface, but are in fact predictable (in principle).

The first type of change is steady change. Change of this sort occurs at a predictable rate. For example, radioactive decay follows a predictable exponential curve. The number of undecayed atoms remaining after a given time in a radioactive sample can be simply calculated if one knows the half-life of the element involved. For example, half of the atoms in any sample will decay in 14.3 days. Similarly, the distance traveled by a car traveling at 55 miles an hour can be simply calculated for any time after the car leaves (assuming it hasn't run out of gas). Another familiar nonscientific example of steady change would be the steady growth of the balance in an untouched savings account: The rules of compound interest acting on the original balance produce a predictable growth in the daily balance of the account.

The second type of change, cyclic change, frequently is found in nature. A partial list of scientifically interesting cycles would include the phases of the moon, the sunspot cycle, the tides, daily cyclic changes in the levels of hormones in the human body, the sleep-wake cycle in animals, and so on. Some of these examples are familiar to nonscientists as well: We all expect the sun to rise in the east and set in the west once a day, and monthly variations in hormone levels have manifestations that are familiar to almost every female human being over the age of about 13. Other familiar cycles include the credit card billing cycle and the annual recurrence of events such as Christmas, Easter, and fund drives on public television.

The third type of change, random change, also is common in nature. Scientific examples would include the occurrence of spontaneous mutations in genes and the radioactive decay of individual atoms. Nobody can predict when a particular gene in a particular organism will undergo mutation, and nobody can tell by looking at a radioactive atom when it will decay. Interestingly enough, though, these processes that are random at the level of the individual gene or atom have definable rates when one looks at all of the genes in a population of animals (the mutation rate) or all of the radioactive atoms in a sample (the half-life). A similar, nonscientific, example would be winning the lottery. Winning the lottery is a random event. Beforehand, nobody can predict who will win; yet the odds of winning are predictable. Again, this is a process that is unpredictable at the individual level but totally predictable at the level of a population of individuals.

One of the most exciting developments in science in the 1980s was the understanding of chaotic change. Chaos occurs when a system obeys completely predictable behavior (i.e., given the exact state of a system at one time, one can determine its exact state at a future time), but our intrinsic lack of knowledge of its initial state causes its future behavior to appear random. Consider the motion of an asteroid, for example. If you knew the exact position and velocity of an asteroid, you could determine its exact position and velocity at any time in the future. However, a small uncertainty (such as a one millimeter uncertainty in its position) will eventually lead to a huge uncertainty in the future. The position of the asteroid in the future will not be determinable, that is, it will appear random. Similarly, if the location of all of the atoms of our atmosphere were perfectly known at one particular time, the weather could be predicted far into the future. The fact that we don't know those locations exactly (e.g., a butterfly flapping its wings in China will disturb some of the atoms) will lead to huge uncertainties in weather prediction; thus, we will likely never be able to predict the weather very far in advance. It might seem that it is difficult to differentiate between random change and chaotic change, but there are very precise mathematical relations followed by chaotic systems. One of the main realizations of the 1980s was that many systems previously thought to be random, such as water turbulence, weather phenomena, and even cardiac ventricular fibrillation, are in fact chaotic. A good nonscientific example of a chaotic process is the stock market's behavior.

Some systems are characterized not by change but by lack of change. These systems are said to be in equilibrium. The unopened bottle of soda on the shelf in the pantry illustrates this concept in several ways. First, it is static, at rest. All of the outside forces acting on it are balanced: Gravity pulling downward on it is balanced by the force that the shelf exerts to hold it up. Second, the amount of water in it is the same as the amount of water placed in it at the bottling plant. The water in the root beer is not static, however, but is in a state of dynamic equilibrium between two phases: water vapor in the little air space in the neck of the bottle and liquid water in the soda below. The important thing that allows this system to remain in equilibrium is that the bottle is closed. When it is closed, the average number of water molecules that evaporate and leave the liquid phase is exactly balanced by the average number of water molecules condensing from the vapor phase into the liquid phase. Once the bottle is opened, this equilibrium vanishes: Water molecules in the vapor phase can and do escape out the neck of the bottle and the water in the bottle will eventually evaporate. In dynamic equilibrium, therefore, a seeming lack of change reflects balanced processes of change occurring within a system.

The state of dynamic equilibrium that exists in a closed root beer bottle does not depend on any outside forces for its maintenance. Other examples of lack of change, though, represent the interposition of regulatory forces on the system. A simple example of such a system is the thermostat-house system. When the temperature in the house drops below a predetermined level, the sensor in the thermostat notices this and causes the furnace to heat the house. Once the house is warm again, the sensor in the thermostat causes the furnace to shut off. The maintenance of a constant temperature in the house is thus dependent on the regulatory behavior of the sensor. Feedback from the sensor keeps the system stable.

Another, more complicated example of regulated constancy is homeostasis: the maintenance of physical stability within an organism. In humans, for example, everything from our body temperature to the concentrations of different ions in our bloodstream remains fairly constant. This reflects tight control exerted by the cells of our body over these systems: regulation that requires constant sensing of the current state of affairs and compensation for changes that occur as we move, eat, sleep, and do all of the other things that humans do. One example of the mechanisms involved in homeostasis is the action of insulin and its function in regulating blood sugar levels. As a carbohydrate-rich meal begins to be absorbed by the body, the amount of glucose in the bloodstream begins to rise. In response to this, insulin is secreted by the pancreas into the bloodstream. Insulin stimulates the liver to take up extra sugar and store it in the form of glycogen (a starch-like substance); it increases the uptake of sugar by muscle cells and its conversion into glycogen; it inhibits the liver from producing glucose from its glycogen stores; and it stimulates muscle and liver cells to "burn" glucose for energy at a more rapid rate. These activities reduce the amount of glucose in the bloodstream, insulin secretion by the pancreas drops, and things are back to normal. The control of blood sugar levels by the body is complicated and requires a great deal of coordination among the different cells of the body.

Rationale for Teaching the Concept

Change is an inescapable feature of both scientific and nonscientific systems; indeed, it is often the most interesting feature of either kind of system. In science, for example, the study of developmental biology is concerned entirely with the mechanisms behind the amazing changes that occur as an organism develops from seed or fertilized egg into its mature form; meteorology concerns itself with atmospheric changes; and much of geology involves the study of the changes that have occurred since the Earth was formed. Outside of science, the daily changes in the stock market are important to millions of investors; changes in the weather matter to essentially everyone; and the changes that occur as a baby grows into an adult fascinate parents, grandparents, and teachers alike. An understanding of the basic types of change, as well as of the concept of equilibrium, is useful for anyone.

Suggested Applications

Many areas of science involve change. Below is a very partial list of suggestions for areas that could be used in illustrating change, equilibrium, and regulation.

Steady Change

Simple physical changes:
- Temperature change in water as it is heated (and what do you see at the freezing and boiling points?)
- Titration of an acid with a base; watch the pH change
- Rates of random change (mutation formation, radioactive decay)

Cyclic Change

- Astronomical phenomena (phases of the moon, seasons, changes in day length over the course of the year, behavior of the tides)
- Biological cycles: life cycles, sleep-wake cycle, opening and closing of flowers in plants over the course of the day, the turning of sunflowers to follow the sun, the menstrual cycle

Random Change

- Radioactive decay
- Spontaneous mutation formation in microbes and man
- Study of probability and statistics

Chaotic Change

As discussed above, chaotic change is change that could in principle be predicted but in fact is unpredictable because of the large numbers of variables involved and uncertainty in measuring starting conditions. Younger children probably have enough difficulty learning that change can be predicted (steady change, cyclic change, rates of random change); introducing chaos at the same time might be confusing. For older children (grades 6–8 or so), the best introduction to chaos would probably be to play with a calculator or computer: Once they have seen the concept in this abstract way, they'll be able to see it in more concrete ways (one of the few cases where hands-on experimentation may *not* be the best way to introduce a new concept!).

Feedback, Control, and Regulation

- Electronics: study systems like thermostats
- Physiology (human and animal)

Appendix B
Teaching Models

Introduction to the Teaching Models

Several teaching models are incorporated into the Project Clarion units. These models ensure emphasis on unit outcomes and support student understanding of the concepts and processes that are the focus of each unit. Teachers should become familiar with these models and how to use them before teaching the unit. The models are listed below and outlined in the pages that follow.
1. Frayer Model of Vocabulary Development
2. Taba Model of Concept Development
3. Concept Mapping
4. Wheel of Scientific Investigation and Reasoning

Frayer Model of Vocabulary Development

The Frayer Model (Frayer, Frederick, & Klausmeier, 1969) provides students with a graphic organizer that asks them to think about and describe the meaning of a word or concept. This process enables them to strengthen their understanding of vocabulary words. Through the model, students are required to consider the important characteristics of the word and to provide examples and nonexamples of the concept. This model has similarities to the Taba Model of Concept Development (1962).

In introducing the Frayer Model to your students, demonstrate its use on large chart paper. Begin with a word all students know, such as rock, umbrella, or shoe, placing it on the graphic model. First, ask the students to define the word in their own words. Record a definition that represents their common knowledge. Next, ask students to give specific characteristics of the word/concept or facts they know about it. Record these ideas. Then ask students to offer examples of the idea and then nonexamples to finish the graphic (see Figure B1).

Another way to use the Frayer Model is to provide students with examples and nonexamples and ask them to consider what word or concept is being analyzed. You can provide similar exercises by filling in some portions of the graphic and asking students to complete the remaining sections.

As students share ideas, note the level of understanding of the group and of individual students. As the unit is taught, certain vocabulary words may need this type of expanded thinking to support student readiness for using the vocabulary in the science activities. You may want students to maintain individual notebooks of words so that they can refer back to them in their work.

Taba Model of Concept Development

Each Project Clarion unit supports the development of a specific macroconcept (change or systems). The concept development model, based upon the work of Hilda Taba (1962), supports student learning of the macroconcept. The model involves both inductive and deductive reasoning processes. Used as an early lesson in the unit, the model focuses on the creation of generalizations about the macroconcept from a student-derived list of created concept examples. The model includes a series

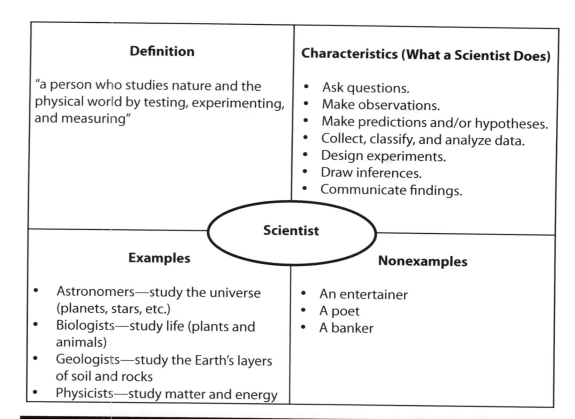

Definition	Characteristics (What a Scientist Does)
"a person who studies nature and the physical world by testing, experimenting, and measuring"	• Ask questions. • Make observations. • Make predictions and/or hypotheses. • Collect, classify, and analyze data. • Design experiments. • Draw inferences. • Communicate findings.
Examples	**Nonexamples**
• Astronomers—study the universe (planets, stars, etc.) • Biologists—study life (plants and animals) • Geologists—study the Earth's layers of soil and rocks • Physicists—study matter and energy	• An entertainer • A poet • A banker

Figure B1. Completed graphic organizer for Frayer Model.

of steps, in which each step involves student participation. Students begin with a broad concept, determine specific examples of the broad concept, create appropriate categorization systems, cite nonexamples of the concept, establish generalizations based on their understanding, and then apply the generalizations to their readings and other situations.

The model generally is most effective when small groups of students work through each step, with whole-class debriefing following each stage of the process. However, with primary-age students, additional teacher guidance may be necessary, especially for the later stages of the model. The steps of the model are outlined below, using the unit concept of change.

1. Students generate examples of the concept of change, derived from their own understanding and experiences with change in the world. Teachers should encourage students to provide at least 15–20 examples; a class list may be created out of the small-group lists to lengthen the set of changes students have to work with.

2. Students then group their changes into categories. This process allows students to search for interrelatedness and to organize their thinking. It often is helpful to have individual examples written on cards so that the categorization may occur physically as well as mentally or in writing. Students should then explain their reasoning for their categorization system and seek clarification from each other as a whole group. Teachers should ensure that all examples have been accounted for in the categorization system established.

3. Students then generate a list of nonexamples of the concept of change. Teachers may begin this step with the direction, "Now list examples of things that *do not change*." Encourage students to think carefully about their

nonexamples and discuss ideas within their groups. Each group should list five to six nonexamples.

4. The students next determine generalizations about the concept of change, using their lists of examples, categories, and nonexamples. Teachers should then share the unit generalizations and relate valid student generalizations to the unit list. Both lists should be posted in the room throughout the course of the unit.

5. During the unit, students are asked to identify specific examples of the generalizations from their own readings, or to describe how the concept applies to a given situation about which they have read. Students also are asked to apply the generalizations to their own writings and their own lives. Several lessons employ a chart that lists several of the generalizations and asks students to supply examples specifically related to the reading or activity of that lesson.

Concept Mapping

A concept map is a graphic representation of one's knowledge on a particular topic. Concept maps support learning, teaching, and evaluation (Novak & Gowin, 1984). Students clarify and extend their own thinking about a topic. Teachers find concept mapping useful for envisioning the scope of a lesson or unit. They also use student-developed concept maps as a way of measuring their progress. Meaningful concept maps often begin with a particular question (focus question) about a topic, event, or object.

Concept maps were developed in 1972 by Dr. Joseph Novak at Cornell University as part of his research about young children's understanding of science concepts. Students were interviewed by researchers who recorded their responses. The researchers sought an effective way to identify changes in students' understanding over time. Novak and his research colleagues began to represent the students' conceptual understanding in concept maps because learning takes place through the assimilation of new concepts and propositions into existing conceptual and propositional frameworks.

Concept maps show concepts and relationships between them. (See the sample concept map in Figure B2.) The concepts are contained within boxes or oval shapes and the connections between concepts are represented by lines with linking words.

Concepts are the students' perceived ideas generalized from particular experiences. Sometimes the concepts placed on the map may contain more than one word. Words placed on the line link words or phrases. The propositions contain two or more concepts connected by linking words or phrases to form a meaningful statement.

The youngest students may view and develop concept maps making basic connections. They may begin with two concepts joined by a linking word. These "sentences" (propositions) become the building blocks for concept maps. Older students may begin to make multiple connections immediately as they develop their maps.

As students map their knowledge base, they begin to represent their conceptual understanding in a hierarchical manner. The broadest, most inclusive concepts often are found at the top of a concept map. More specific concepts and examples then follow.

Each Project Clarion unit contains an overview concept map, showing the essential knowledge included in the lessons and the connections students should be able to make as a result of their experiences within the unit. This overview may be useful as a classroom poster that the teacher and students may refer to throughout the unit.

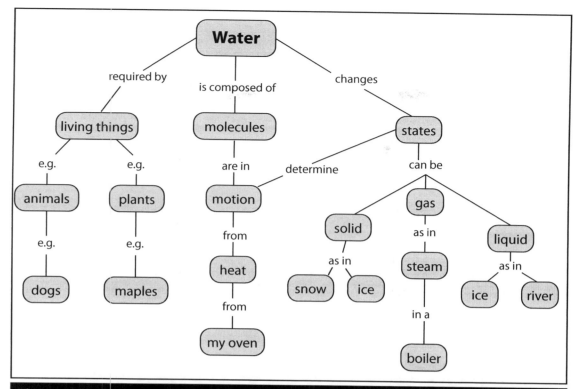

Figure B2. A concept map showing a student's understanding of water.

Note. Adapted from Novak and Gowin (1984).

Strategies to Prepare Students for Concept Mapping

The following strategies can be incorporated to help prepare your students for concept mapping activities (Novak & Gowin, 1984).

What Do Words Mean?

1. Ask students to picture in their minds some common words (e.g., water, tree, door, box, pencil, dog). Start with "object" words, saying them one at a time, allowing time for students to picture each of them.
2. Create a class list of object words, asking students to name other objects they can picture in their minds to add to the list.
3. Next create a list of event words (e.g., jumping, running, eating). Ask students to envision each of these in their minds and encourage them to contribute to the class list of event words.
4. Give students a few words that are likely to be unfamiliar to most of them, asking if they can see a picture in their mind. These words should be short (e.g., data, cell, prey, inertia). You might include a few simple words in another language. Ask students if they have any mind pictures.
5. Discuss the fact that words are useful to us because they convey meaning. This only happens when people can form a picture in their mind that represents the meaning they connect with the word.

What Is a Concept?

1. Introduce the word *concept* and explain that concept is the word we use to mean some kind of object or event we can picture in our mind. Refer back to the word lists previously developed as you discuss the word and ask if these are concepts. Can students see a picture in their mind for each of them? Let students know that when they come upon a word they do not know well enough to form a picture, they will just need to learn the concept associated with that new word.
2. Provide each table with picture cards and ask students to take turns at their table naming some of the concepts included in the card.

What Are Linking Words?

1. Prepare a list of words such as *the, is, are, when, that, then*. Ask students if they can see a picture in their mind for each of these words. Explain that these are not concept words. These are linking words we use when we speak or write to link concept words together into sentences that have special meaning. Ask students if they have any words to add to the list. Label the list "Linking Words."
2. Hold up two picture cards (sky and blue) and give students a sample sentence ("The sky is blue.") Ask students to tell you the concept words and the linking words in your sentence. Give another example.
3. Give each pair of students a few picture cards. Ask the students to work with partners to pick up two cards and then develop a sentence that links the two cards. They should take turns, with one partner making the sentence and the other identifying the concepts and the linking words. Ask them to repeat this a few times and then have several partners share their sentences.
4. Explain to students that it is easy to make up sentences and to read sentences where the printed labels (words) are familiar to them. Explain that reading and writing sentences is like making a link between two things (concepts) they already know. Practice this idea during reading time, asking students to find a sentence and analyze it for concepts and linking words.

Wheel of Scientific Investigation and Reasoning

All scientists work to improve our knowledge and understanding of the world. In the process of scientific inquiry, scientists connect evidence with logical reasoning. Scientists also apply their imaginations as they devise hypotheses and explanations that make sense of the evidence. Students can strengthen their understanding of particular science topics through investigations that cause them to employ evidence gathering, logical reasoning, and creativity. The Wheel of Scientific Investigation and Reasoning contains the specific processes involved in scientific inquiry to guide students' thinking and actions.

Make Observations

Scientists make careful observations and try things out. They must describe things as accurately as possible so that they can compare their observations from one time to another and so that they can compare their observations with those of other scientists. Scientists use their observations to form questions for investigation.

Ask Questions

Scientific investigations usually are initiated through a problem to be solved or a question asked. Selecting just the right question or clearly defining the problem to be addressed is critical to the investigation process.

Learn More

To clarify their questions, scientists learn more by reviewing bodies of scientific knowledge documented in text and previously conducted investigations. Also, when scientists get conflicting information they make fresh observations and insights that may result in revision of the previously formed question. By learning more, scientists can design and conduct more effective experiments or build upon previously conducted experiments.

Design and Conduct the Experiment

Scientists use their collection of relevant evidence, their reasoning, and their imagination to develop a hypothesis. Sometimes scientists have more than one possible explanation for the same set of observations and evidence. Often when additional observations and testing are completed, scientists modify current scientific knowledge.

To test out hypotheses, scientists design experiments that will enable them to control conditions so that their results will be reliable. Scientists repeat their experiments, doing it the same way it was done before and expecting to get very similar, although not exact, results. It is important to control conditions in order to make comparisons. Scientists sometimes are not sure what will happen because they don't know everything that might be having an effect on the experiment's outcome.

Create Meaning

Scientists analyze the data that are collected from the experiment to add to the existing body of scientific knowledge. They organize their data using data tables and graphs and then make inferences from the data to draw conclusions about whether their question was answered and the effectiveness of their experiments. Scientists also create meaning by comparing what they found to existing knowledge. The analysis of data often leads to identification of related questions and future experiments.

Tell Others What Was Found

In the investigation process, scientists often work as a team, sharing findings with each other so that they may benefit from the results. Initially, individual team members complete their own work and draw their own conclusions.

One way to introduce the wheel to students is to provide them with the graphic model (see Figure B3) and ask them to tell one reason why each section of the wheel is important to scientific investigation.

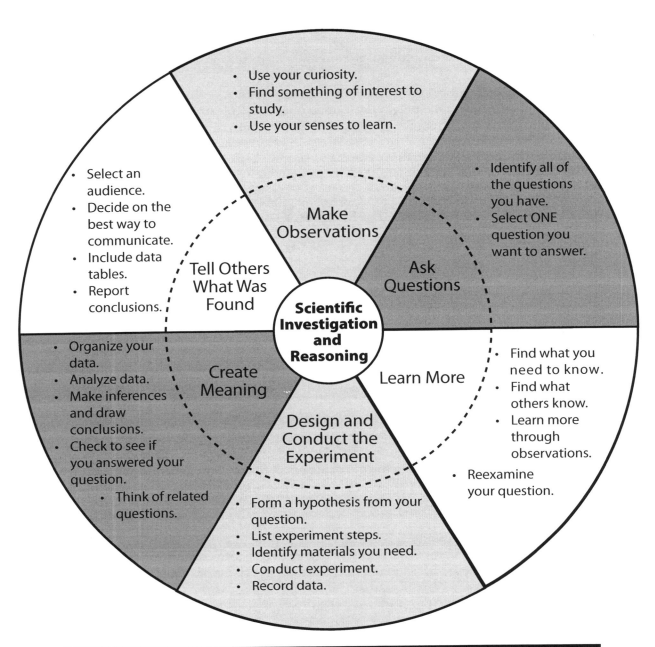

Figure B3. Wheel of Scientific Investigation and Reasoning model.

Note. Adapted from Kramer (1987).

Appendix C
Materials List

Lesson	Materials
Lesson 1: **What Is a** **Scientist?**	• Lab coat for teacher • One lab coat (white adult T-shirt or dress shirt) for each student • Beaker • Microscope • Prepared PowerPoint slides or transparencies of Handout 1A (Completed Frayer Model of Vocabulary Development on Scientists) and Handout 1B (Incomplete Frayer Model of Vocabulary Development on Scientists) • One copy of Handout 1B (Incomplete Frayer Model of Vocabulary Development on Scientists) for each group of three or four students • Markers or pens • One piece of chart paper • Student log books • Blank nametags • *What Is a Scientist?* by Barbara Lehn
Lesson 2: **What Is Change?**	• One pack of sticky notes per each group of three to four students • Chart paper for each group of three to four students, with Handout 2A printed or drawn on it (Taba Concept Model for Change) • Markers • A large class poster of Handout 2A • Four sentence strips with different change generalizations written on each strip • Strawberry or cherry Kool-Aid® • Pitcher of water • Drinking glass (needs to be glass) • Metal object (e.g., spoon) • Food coloring
Lesson 3: **What Scientists** **Do**	• Lab coat for teacher • One lab coat for each student • One feather for each group • One cardboard tube for each group (i.e., paper towel tube), cut into small rings • Clear tape for each group • One length of string for each group (all the same length) • One small battery-operated fan or hair dryer for each group • One stopwatch for each group • Student log books • Charts or slides of Handouts 3A (Wheel of Scientific Investigation and Reasoning), 3B (Small-Group Observations of Wind Sources), 3C (Wind Classifications Blank Concept Map), and 3D (Wind Classifications Completed Concept Map) • Student copies or charts (if using small groups) of Handouts 3A, 3B, and 3C • Markers or pens for students • Sentence strip with the question, "Which type of wind energy will move the feather along the strip the fastest?" • Rulers or yardsticks (optional)
Lesson 4: **Preservation Park**	• *Common Ground: The Water, Earth, and Air We Share* by Molly Bang • Handout 4A (Message From Geologist #1), recorded on tape • Slide of Handout 4B (Need to Know Board) • Chart paper • Markers • Handout 3D, for reference
Lesson 5: **Natural** **Resources, Part I**	• *Brother Eagle, Sister Sky* by Susan Jeffers, or *A Drop Around the World* by Barbara McKinney • Slide of Handout 5A (Concept Definition Map) • Slide of Handout 5B (Need to Know Board: Natural Resources) • Copies of Handouts 5A and 5B, one per group • Student log books • Word for word wall: natural resources

Lesson	Materials
Lesson 6: **Natural** **Resources, Part II**	• *Agatha's Feather Bed: Not Just Another Wild Goose Story* by Carmen Agra Deedy • Slide of Handout 5A (Concept Definition Map), one copy per group of students • Slide of Handout 5B (Need to Know Board: Natural Resources), one copy per group • Poster board, one piece per group • Markers, colored pencils, and other art supplies • Resources for student research (e.g., textbooks, library books, Internet access, articles) on natural resources • Chart paper or slide of Handout 6A (Renewable vs. Nonrenewable T-Chart) • Student log books • Copies of Handout 6B (Natural Resources Blank Concept Map) for each student • Handout 6C (Natural Resources Completed Concept Map) • United Streaming video clip: *Natural Resources* (11 minutes; optional)
Lesson 7: **Renewable** **Energy Resources**	• Slide or chart of Handout 7A (Energy Sources: Advantages and Disadvantages) • Slide or chart of Handout 3A (Wheel of Scientific Investigation and Reasoning) • Bottles painted white and black, one each per group • Small latex balloons of the same size and color, one balloon per bottle (*Note:* The balloons can be any color, but you need to use the same color balloon on both bottles to control this variable.) • A sunny day or a lamp to substitute for the sun (*Note:* Be advised that this experiment works better with actual sunlight.) • Student log books • Words for word wall: renewable energy, nonrenewable energy, solar energy • *My Light* by Molly Bang (optional) • United Streaming video clip: *The Magic School Bus: Getting Energized* (22 minutes; optional)

Lesson 8:
What Is Soil,
Anyway?
	• One small bag per group, labeled Samples A, B, C, D, and E, respectively, of the following:
	  • Sand
	  • Clay (can use modeling clay as substitute if necessary)
	  • Silt (can use chalk dust as substitute if necessary)
	  • Rocks and gravel
	  • Topsoil (potting soil)
	• Wide-mouth jar (e.g., pickle jar, large mayonnaise jar) or small fish bowl, one per group
	• Magnifying glasses
	• Copies of Handout 8A (Characteristics of Soil), one per student or group
	• Copies of Handout 8B (Definitions of Soil Types), one per student or group
	• Copies of Handout 8C (Layers of Soil), one per student or group
	• Copies of Handout 8D (Soil Layers Blank Concept Map), one per student or group
	• Copies of Handout 8E (Soil Layers Completed Concept Map), one per student or group
	• Student log books

Lesson 9: **Soil, Water, and** **Plants**	• One sample of rocks/gravel, clay, sand, and topsoil (potting soil) per group • Four wide-mouth jars per group • Filter paper • Pitcher of water, one per group • Graduated beaker or measuring cup, one per group • Potted plant (for demonstration) • Large jar (for demonstration—should be large enough for the class to see when it is in the front of the room) • Small spade • Slide of Handout 3A (Wheel of Scientific Investigation and Reasoning) • Slide of Handout 9A (Soil Types Blank Concept Map) • Slide of Handout 9B (Soil Types Completed Concept Map) • Copies of Handouts 9A and 9B, one per student • Student log books • Word for word wall: humus

Lesson	Materials
Lesson 10: **Soil Erosion**	• Handout 10A (Message From Geologist #2), recorded on tape • Slide of Handout 3A (Wheel of Scientific Investigation and Reasoning) • Two large aluminum pans full of soil • One large aluminum pan, empty • Scissors • Several large books • Twigs with leaves to use as trees and plants • Other objects to use as barriers to erosion (choose versatile items that could represent a number of student suggestions) • Hair dryer • Watering can full of water • Extra water (if you don't have a sink in your classroom) • Student log books • United Streaming video clip: *Geologist's Notebook: Making a Mud Pie* (11 minutes). • Word for word wall: erosion
Lesson 11: **Land Pollution:** **Garbage!**	• *Where Does the Garbage Go?* by Paul Showers • Slide and one copy per student of Handout 11A (Garbage Data Collection Table) • Plastic drop cloth • Signs labeled "Food and Yard Waste," "Glass," "Metal," "Paper," "Plastic," and "Other" • Plastic gloves, one pair for each student • Large bag of nonhazardous garbage (collect trash from neighboring classrooms for a few days) • Six garbage bags • Bathroom scale • Markers • "Sarah Cynthia Sylvia Stout Would Not Take the Garbage Out" by Shel Silverstein • Student log books
Lesson 12: **Oil Spill!**	• *Oil Spill!* by Melvin Berger • Slide of Handout 3A (Scientific Wheel of Investigation and Reasoning) • Copies of Handout 12A (Oil Spill Cleanup Experiment Log), one per student • Copies of Handout 12B (Experimental Report Form), one per student • Small disposable pans, four per group with each separately labeled "water," "A," "B," and "C" • Containers of water at room temperature, one per group • Containers of vegetable oil, one per group • Drop cloth (or sufficient newspaper) to place under pans, one per group • Roll of paper towels, one per group • Containers of liquid dish soap, one per group • Containers of baking soda, one per group • Feathers (craft or real), 12–15 per group • Plastic spoons, two per group (to measure dish soap and baking soda) • Student log books • Scientific Investigation Badges, one per student printed on colored paper or labels and laminated (optional)
Lesson 13: **Planning** **Preservation Park**	• *Someday a Tree* by Eve Bunting • Handout 13A (Message From Geologist #3), previously recorded • Scratch paper and/or graph paper • Poster board or trifold boards, one per group • Markers, colored pencils, glue, paint, and other art supplies • Student log books
Lesson 14: **Preservation** **Park Planning** **Committee**	• Group posters or trifolds • Copies of Handout 14A (Presentation Rubric) • Handout 14B (Preservation Expert Badges), copied on color paper or labels and laminated (optional)
Lesson 15: **Wrap It Up!**	• Student log books • Chart paper • Markers • Small plant • Cup, large enough to cover the plant and that will enclose the plant in darkness • Copies of Handout 12B (Experimental Report Form), or slide for class viewing

References

Center for Science, Mathematics, and Engineering Education. (1996). *National science education standards.* Washington, DC: National Academy Press.

Fowler, M. (1990). The diet cola test. *Science Scope, 13,* 32–34.

Frayer, D. A., Frederick, W. C., & Klausmeier, H. J. (1969). *A schema for testing the level of concept mastery.* Working paper from the Wisconsin Research and Development Center for Cognitive Learning, The University of Wisconsin.

Kramer, S. P. (1987). *How to think like a scientist: Answering questions by the scientific method.* New York: T. Y. Crowell.

Mineral Information Institute. (2007). *300 million Americans need 7 billion tons to maintain living standard.* Retrieved from http://www.mii.org/pdfs/2007_mii_Baby_Info.pdf

Novak, J., & Gowin, B. D. (1984). *Learning how to learn.* New York: Cambridge University Press.

Scholastic. (1996). *Scholastic children's dictionary* (Rev. ed.). New York: Author.

Sher, B. T. (2004). Change. In J. L. VanTassel-Baska (Ed.), *Science key concepts* (pp. 31–35). Williamsburg, VA: Center for Gifted Education, College of William and Mary.

Taba, H. (1962). *Curriculum: Theory and practice.* New York: Harcourt Brace.

VanTassel-Baska, J. (1986). Effective curriculum and instructional models for talented students. *Gifted Child Quarterly, 30,* 164–169.

VanTassel-Baska, J., & Little, C. (Eds.). (2003). *Content-based curriculum for gifted learners.* Waco, TX: Prufrock Press.